Give a F**k

A brief inventory of ways in which you can

FELICITY MORSE

ixia
PRESS

Mineola, New York

Bibliographical Note

This Ixia Press edition, first published in 2019, is a republication of the work published in Great Britain by Michael O'Mara Books, Ltd, London, in 2018.

International Standard Book Number

ISBN-13: 978-0-486-83593-8
ISBN-10: 0-486-83593-6

Ixia Press
An imprint of Dover Publications, Inc.

Manufactured in the United States by LSC Communications
835936   2019
www.doverpublications.com/ixiapress

CONTENTS

A BATTLE OF F**KS | 5

Yourself

GIVE A F**K ABOUT YOURSELF | 13
ABOUT RIGHT NOW **15** HOW TO TALK TO YOURSELF **25**
FEELINGS **32** STORYTELLING **41** YOUR BODY **50**
MOVEMENT **55** REST **61** DRINKING, SMOKING, DRUGS **66**
SKIN TIME **71** FOOD **76** NATURE **86** IMAGINATION **91**

Relationships

GIVE A F**K ABOUT RELATIONSHIPS | 101
BOUNDARIES **103** OWNING YOUR PART **122**
GETTING OFF YOUR HIGH HORSE **127** VICTIMHOOD **131**
BLAME **137** SHAME **142** HONESTY **147** BEING UNCONDITIONAL **156**
GIVING **163** RECEIVING **170** SEX **177** COMMUNITY **189** WORK **209**
SOCIAL MEDIA **220** WHERE YOU LIVE **235**

Infinity and Beyond

GIVE A F**K ABOUT INFINITY AND BEYOND | 249
THE NEWS **253** MONEY **267** PURPOSE **280** YOUR WORLDVIEW **290**
PLUGGING INTO THE BIGGER PICTURE **306**

ACKNOWLEDGMENTS | 317

NOTES | 318

A BATTLE OF F**KS

Here's the truth: There are times when being a sensitive, caring human being sucks. This world can be a difficult place to navigate, and if you not only feel all of its pain, but want to change it for the better, then it's easy to become overwhelmed, burn out, or even check out altogether.

Whether we're aware of it or not, most of us are engaged in a philosophical struggle as we go about our daily lives. It is a fight I have come to see as "a battle of f**ks." Forget "to be or not to be" in this golden age of interconnected agitation, post-Trump, post-Brexit, with so many overwhelming demands on our attention, the existential question we face is whether or not to give an actual f**k.

It's a question I've sat with for a long time. Working in news for the best part of the last decade, first as a journalist, then as a social media producer, and finally as an editor, my daily diet was once the world's calamities. There were cheery stories, too, of course, but it is the terrible ones that are burnt on my mind: the distressing images and footage; humanity facing unimaginable pain and conflict. Empathy is unavoidable—and exhausting. There comes a point where caring feels just too much.

So I understand if in this battle, you'd rather just say "F**k it!" and withdraw into your own comfortable little sphere, murmuring only a cursory "Isn't it terrible?" at dinner parties. A life where all you really give a f**k about is reclining on the sofa with a large glass of wine and forgetting about the world's woes, because what could you do about them anyway?

Perhaps this isn't you, but you know of someone a bit like this, though their "f**k it" attitude might be dressed a bit differently, in smug pseudo-spiritual garb. You'll identify these folks by their complacent virtue-signaling smile, their faraway look while you try and engage them with the world, only to be advised that "letting go" or "taking life less seriously" is the way forward. It's not that I'm unaware of the spiritual benefits of "surrender"; it's just that this meditative attitude—though wonderful while "omming" on the mountaintop—is not much use to those of us who live down below in the marketplace and are continually aware of the utter state of things. Letting go is only the first part of any process—we actually need to pick the important stuff back up again and learn how to care about it so that things move and change.

We are part of this world—it affects *us* and we affect *it*—it is inevitable that we care: it is natural and it is right. We're challenged by the difficulty of how to do this without ending up enrolling as a member of another passionate tribe—the worrier cadets—a bunch made inactive by the sheer scale of their concern about everything. They aren't much fun to be around, and their hyperactive cousins, sometimes admirable project managers, can be equally annoying in their evangelism.

You may or may not recognize yourself among some of these stereotypes. In reality, most of us tend to switch sides fairly regularly, depending on how overwhelmed, irritated, or exhausted we feel. Neither way quite fits the demands of modern life, so the majority of us ping-pong between the two, watching our newsfeeds, putting in overtime at work, and, occasionally, becoming imbued with a sense of justice and purpose. Until it all gets too much. Then we become wired and tired and pop off for a nap, that glass of wine, or a yoga class. We become rested and then begin to care again, and so the cycle continues.

At some point, even the cycle itself becomes ennui-inducing, and we slowly disengage altogether, living a smaller, more convenient life. Then we aren't even challenged by the discomfort of what to give a f★★k about, as everything has been arranged to be wonderfully comfortable. We haven't found the answer, so we stop even asking the question, dismissing the activity as worthless.

I have joyfully, miserably, painfully, energetically, exhaustedly tried to live my life in all of these arrangements. I have repeatedly floundered and f★★ked up. I have clawed my way back up to the top of the cliff edge, humiliated but fighting, only to be knocked out by yet another falling boulder (this was an emotional battle—I'm actually not very athletic). In 2015, I reached rock bottom. There wasn't anything dramatic that took me there. I wish there had been; that would have been a good story to tell. It was just the culmination of a thousand little, emotional mosquito bites that I finally woke up to and decided that I couldn't live with anymore.

Finding myself in this unbearable spot, I had to do something about it. I did a lot of unhelpful and unhealthy things for some time before I started becoming interested in personal development programs, enrolling in a number of courses, a process that led me to become a life coach alongside writing. As part of this, I discovered that in the battle of f**ks, there is a middle way—that you really can care about the important stuff without losing your mind.

You'll know if you've met someone who truly "cares"; just by talking to them you'll feel inspired and energetic—suddenly everything feels charged with possibility. It's contagious. Who wouldn't want to be that type of person?

Honing our ability to be caring and curious honors our time here on Earth and gives our lives meaning. It makes the world a better place too. Being conscious of our own existence, staying present with our experiences, and learning about the world so that things happen for us, not to us, is a transformative process.

Like anything worthwhile, it's easier saying it than doing it. But it's all about the doing. See, proper caring is actually a practice. Think of it like a muscle. And as with all training, you need to start small to avoid getting whacked. Lots of us are starting too big with our give-a-f**k muscle—picking up the 100 lb. weight (say, for example, starvation in Africa)—

and then deciding it's too heavy for us because we couldn't pick it up successfully. We become disillusioned.

Or perhaps we soldier on regardless, but ultimately pretty pointlessly. How many people do you know who are campaigning for a cause but you feel their attention would be better directed closer to home?

Many of us have also picked up the habit of only really paying attention to the things we are strongly for or against. We give a lot of thought to the things that we hate or annoy us: that woman who won't shut up at work, or how late the bus is, or the way our partner always leaves the seat up. Then we forget about our lovely colleague who always makes our coffee just right, and the weather is not too bad either—and aren't the colors of that tree's leaves rather beautiful? Conversely, only focusing on things we love makes us avoidant, turning our attention away from our fears, confrontation, or anything that threatens us and telling ourselves and people around us that we "don't really give a f★★k."

Think about what's behind not caring. Perhaps spouting provocatively on social media, for example, is exposing that what you *really* long for is human connection. Maybe complaining about your job is a hidden way of saying that you just want to feel fulfilled? We can use what we *don't want* to show us what we do want. Anger often lies underneath fear, and below fear there is usually something we love that we are trying to protect. Clearing surface obstacles and finding out what we truly care about allows us to get in touch with ourselves.

Admitting you care is a scary minirebellion. People think admitting to your fears is hard, but often it's actually expressing what you want or need that's the most challenging and courageous part. Caring is hard. But if you fail at first, don't worry. This journey you're going on is not about beating yourself up—it's about embracing things and discovering yourself, and doing it with care.

I'm a BIG proponent of giving a f**k. I firmly believe that it not only empowers you, it empowers your family, your community, and, if you do it right, the sky's the limit.

What I've learned so far has been transformative when it comes to my mental health, my happiness, my relationships, my community—and my power to effect change in the wider world. I hope that this book will bring some of that transformation your way.

Commit to caring and the possibility of making a positive difference in this chaotic world opens right up. When you align yourself with your values, the things you care about, you not only discover more about yourself, you also reclaim your purpose and naturally discover where your true desire lies.

Caring involves being interested, being curious, in all aspects of life. It's about directing your attention, embracing the pleasant and the unpleasant, and considering what it gives you and what you can do.

Consider me your give-a-f**k personal trainer.

Felicity Morse

Yourself

GIVE A F**K ABOUT YOURSELF

It's not selfish to care about yourself. In fact it's more narrow-minded not to. The world needs you fully alive, awake, happy, and nourished, and for that you need to first and foremost give a f★★k about you.

This means fostering a deep acceptance, love, and care for yourself and making sure you make enough space in your life for your vital needs. The demands of your body, your mind, your heart. How else will you learn how to comfort others if you don't even know how to gracefully attend to the requests of your own sweet self?

There appears to be current confusion in the media between self-care and "pampering," with the concept of "self-care" seemingly used to sell a lot of often expensive products or experiences. Self-care is not (just) about getting a pedicure, a massage, or perfect skin forever; it's more fundamental than that. It's an attitude toward oneself that says: "I deserve to be here … I may be flawed, I may be fallible, but I'm just like everyone else, and I deserve to take up space on this planet." Lovely though it is, there is no amount of pampering that can make up for a belief that you're worthless, that there is something wrong with you, that you're a f**k-up or undeserving of love—even your own.

If you have these negative beliefs about yourself, they can be intensely painful (believe me, I've been there), but in truth they are a bit arrogant too. What makes you so awful, different, and detestable compared to the rest of the human race? What's so special about you that makes you any less deserving of living on this planet? Nurturing a kinder attitude toward ourselves doesn't happen overnight. Sometimes we need a template to help us get there, which is what this section hopes to provide. Self-care is an attitude, but it's also reflected in our behavior. When you value yourself, you respect your body and your mind, attending to their needs and what gives them pleasure with all the loving-kindness that lives inside of you. You do this no matter what sort of day you've had—or how much you've f**ked up. You do this because you know you have intrinsic value as a human, and you don't need to do a bunch of things before you can allow yourself to be happy. It was French philosopher Pierre Teilhard de Chardin who said, "We are not human beings having a *spiritual* experience. We are spiritual beings having a human experience."[1]

Caring about yourself is a constantly evolving process—it's not that you have to "complete" self-love before you can interact with the world. All your experiences in relationships and community can act as practice to help you love yourself.

Some people think that the way we see the world reflects how we relate with ourselves. If there are parts of ourselves we have abandoned or rejected, we will judge and become intolerant of them in others. If we are angry at ourselves, we become angry with the world. Similarly, the things we admire in others are qualities we recognize in ourselves but may not have acknowledged yet—though they are latent within us. Giving a f★★k about yourself in this way is a process of reclaiming the greatness within you and displaying it in your own unique way.

The headings throughout this book are intended to help give you a structure from which, if self-love is still a work in progress, you have a better springboard to get there. Just the willingness to live this way is a loving act in itself. Adopting the behaviors and thinking suggested have helped me remember in darker times that actually I'm pretty nice and worth looking after. I hope now that I've remembered I can help you remember your awesomeness too. Then, when you see someone struggling, you can do the same for them.

About Right Now

Checking in with the present moment regularly is as good as any relaxation retreat on the market. Forget colonic irrigation in the Caribbean, the "right now" is an energetic pit stop, and it's a trampoline for the future. If you can face it and be in it—honestly and objectively—then it helps you to set your compass effectively toward where you want to be.

It's fun getting so excited about the future (I call these moments of high energy "possibility parties") that you sprint toward the destination, fixated on a fantasy. But it doesn't always work if you ignore reality as it is. A map is simply a pretty picture if you can't plot where you are on it accurately.

Trust me, I know.

Some Saturday mornings, while I'm sipping my first cup of coffee, I'm filled with a very strong sense that I might just be able to save the world. I'm post–sleeping in, there's sunshine streaming through the blinds, and the entire weekend sprawls before me. Clear, energized, and imbued with my own brilliance, I want to use my (God-given) talents to serve the world.

I could bake a showstopping cake or begin a community cookout project. I might get invited on the news, winning wide acclaim. I could pitch my philosophy to international thought leaders. I might start a movement; I could write an erudite and witty Facebook post about it—I bet it would go viral. Gosh, I could end up running for office. My power would be limitless. I bet I could even clean the bathroom.

Fast-forward forty-five minutes. Bleach slowly slugs its way out of an overturned bottle onto the bathroom floor. Paper towels are everywhere. The smoke alarm is going off due to the burning cake. The dog has used the brief interlude in which I extinguished the cake to steal a used tampon from the garbage can.

As I chase him, the belt loops of my dressing gown get hooked onto the kitchen door handle and I fall into a tangled heap. Still attached to the kitchen door, I check social media. Approximately five people have liked the inspirational quote I posted on Facebook. Over in the hallway, the dog is enthusiastically eating the used feminine hygiene product. Le sigh.

Forget saving the world—it is questionable whether I can even save myself.

You might be fortunate enough never to have found yourself in this exact scenario, but most of us can relate to a situation where we started a few different things, full of good intentions, but forgot to factor in the reality part. Things didn't pan out as expected. Other people got involved. Circumstances started competing for our attention. We began feeling like we were spinning lots of plates. If our minds were internet browsers, we'd have thirty-five different tabs open simultaneously, and maybe an annoying pop-up video in the bottom right-hand corner.

It's tempting to say "F★★k it," walk away, switch off. Give up on what you want and give up doing anything to get it. Say you're not good enough, the world is f★★ked up, and it's hopeless.

Returning to the right now is the antidote to that.

When my mind starts spinning out of control, I bring myself back to the present. Land myself, consciously, in my body and in my mind, in what is going on and how I am feeling right now. Some people check into a luxury hotel to relax; I check in with myself, right there in the moment (because not only am I a smartass, I'm also a cheapskate).

So, before you get any further, stop for a second and make friends with where you are and what's going on for you right now, and just appreciate it for what it is.

★ Take a deep breath, in through your nose and out through your mouth. Acknowledge that it might feel uncomfortable to slow down. Sit with that feeling. It's okay. It's a sign that now is the perfect time to check in with yourself and the right now.

★ Can you let the skin on your face relax? Let your tongue lie thick and heavy in your mouth? Have your shoulders sunk down? Is your belly relaxed?

★ Now begin to notice. Start with three things you can see. They can be mundane: this book, that chair, the window in front of you.

★ Press your index finger and thumb together as you name them under your breath.

★ Then focus your attention a little more. Notice three things you can hear. It might be traffic. Or birdsong in the distance. The sky might be grumbling; perhaps you can hear wind and rain. Maybe people are talking—there's a low-level murmur. Listen.

★ Press your middle finger and thumb together as you name them under your breath.

★ Finally, notice three things you can feel. Maybe the texture of the book under your fingers. Or the feeling of whatever you are sitting or lying on. Perhaps it's the feeling of your feet on the ground, in your shoes, or the air on your face.

★ Press your ring finger and thumb together as you silently name what you can feel.

You can do this exercise—three things you can see, three things you can hear, three things you can feel—every time stuff starts to feel too much.

A lot of us spend our days doing two or three things at once while half-living an imagined version of the future and occasionally analyzing the past. That's a lot of mental effort expended on fighting reality. Living in the right now from time to time saves energy, freeing up more headspace—and, with it, more concentration.

We can harness the extra attention to focus on what we really want and what is the best way to get there, taking the complexities of the current situation into account. Or maybe it turns out that, without all the extra noise, the right now is actually pretty great.

Forcing the Future Ends in Failure

We all want things. However, sometimes we get so fixated on the "how" and the "what"—especially if a certain blueprint was successful in the past or has proved fruitful for others—that we end up missing terrific opportunities.

Blockbuster's CEO passed up the chance to buy Netflix for $50 million. Would Blockbuster have gone bust if he'd taken a moment to check in with what was going on in the right now with changing technologies?

It's not just businesses that fall victim to this kind of thinking. A lot of us become unwilling to adapt to changing circumstances. A detailed plan can quickly turn into tunnel vision. We become overly attached not just to what we want to happen, but to exactly how that thing is going to happen and what it's going to look like. I call it trying to force the future.

It's easy to say that Blockbuster should have seen it coming, but I know that, in more than one situation, I've been so absorbed in what I think should happen, or what I desperately want to happen, that I've missed what actually was happening. This result was more mess and pain than it needed to be.

It used to happen to me often when I was dating. The evidence was all there that we weren't right for each other, but I was so fixated on what I wanted to happen that I ignored all the signs, getting off on my bridal-suite fairy tale of what our future could hold. Sure, it was too uncomfortable to confront the truth of the situation and realize I wasn't happy, but it was even messier to wake up nine months down the line in crisis about it.

> Our minds can attend to 126 pieces of information per second—there's always more we can pay attention to in the right now.[2]

I'm not suggesting you should just quit if a situation or a relationship isn't perfect right away. I'm saying you have to tackle "what is" rather than what you want it to be in order to move forward. This applies to so many things. We don't face the right now of our finances. We spend time in friendships that have gone stale or make us feel bad. We ignore the health of our bodies and stick around for years moaning about a job, just hoping it will change. We resist the right now because it's painful or it doesn't feel like it's where we want to be. Yet when we can't accept the situation as it truly is, we create drama for ourselves and others in the long term.

There's also the chance that, maybe, once we slow down and come into the now, once we stop trying to get anywhere at all and accept the situation as it is, we find out that where we are feels pretty damn good and we could stop and think about just appreciating that for a minute.

Snakes and Ladders

"Right now" isn't always rosy. Accepting "what is" is especially bruising if, like me, you prefer feeling as though you are constantly making progress. I'm not sure who first gave me the idea that from birth to death there should be some sense of continual forward movement, but if I do meet the aforementioned individual, I will tell them I feel deeply misled.

Life feels more like a game of snakes and ladders: sometimes you roll the dice and move forward steadily; other times, you roll a few ladders and breakthroughs happen rapidly. Being in the right now at that point is easy. Hurrah!

Then, perhaps just as you feel you're on a winning streak, right up ahead, you roll a snake and slide down a few places. Then you meet another snake, and then another, and before you know it, it feels like you're almost back at the beginning, way out on your own. If that's your right now, I understand. I've been there.

At those times, remember that *all we have* is the present moment, and that there are always more resources available to you than you think—both on the outside and on the inside—once you've wiped the tears away.

This Moment Matters

Being present in the right now, and allowing yourself to feel what is going on for you in the moment you are in, is in itself an act of bravery. We're talking about confronting the brutal facts of life now, folks—and choosing to go on in spite of that, because you are willing to believe that there's something better and that you will get there in the end.

Even if right now is uncomfortable, it matters—perhaps even more so. How did you end up here? What needs to change? What can you learn from this moment?

Hold in your heart the knowledge that it's not always possible or necessary to be aware of the exact route you're taking somewhere—you can still be victorious. Life is not always linear. Who am I to say that getting a snake and falling down right now won't mean I'll end up on a long ladder in a few rolls? Maybe if I didn't roll a snake, I wouldn't be able to climb that long ladder? This moment will matter in ways you can't imagine yet.

If you've rolled a snake recently, here's what I do. I confront the present reality, with its lipstick and eyeliner off, then I look around and ask myself what the next thing I could do right now to move me forward might be. And I roll the dice. And after I've moved forward a few places, I look around, take stock, and ask myself what the next right step might be. It doesn't all have to happen on a sunny Saturday morning.

Then, step by step, you arrive where you want to be—sometimes sooner than you expected.

That's the funny thing about sustainable change. It doesn't look quite the way we expect. Sometimes, it doesn't feel like you're moving at all, which can be frustrating if, like me, you love seeing progress.

At those times I think of it like a flower blooming. You don't notice growth taking place, until suddenly you walk past a tree on your road and you're, like, "Wow, the blossom is out." As if it happened suddenly, all in one fell swoop. But really it's been lots of things coming together slowly, step by tiny step, imperceptibly, until then magic happens.

Acknowledge the Good Stuff

When we're checking in with the present, it's also important to take stock of all the good things we have received and achieved. Often, we discount them in favor of focusing on an obstacle, but without acknowledging the solid bits underneath and behind us, we have no foundation from which we can climb mountains. Plus, half the fun is how you get there—life does not need to be a relentless, joyless race toward some spurious notion of success. You are allowed to enjoy life, even if you haven't done everything on your to-do list.

Sometimes when I'm checking in with right now, and feel like at this moment my reality is brutal, I make a list. I write "Right Now" at the top, then create two columns underneath. In one column I write "Good Things" and in the other column I write "Bad Things."

Sometimes I just start the list of Good Things with "I'm alive." It's a decent beginning. As Jon Kabat-Zinn writes in *Full Catastrophe Living*, "As long as you are breathing, there is more right with you than there is wrong, no matter how ill or how hopeless you may feel."[3]

None of us knows what will happen tomorrow. Every twenty-four hours that pass, the clock ticks past the exact time of the day that (hopefully far in the future) I will die. Checking in with my "death anniversary" is something I choose to remember in my most irritable, frustrated moments. This morbid thought is not meant to send you spiraling into bleakness; it's just a gentle reminder to live in the moment. To appreciate what you can, however messy that looks right now.

So yes, this moment matters. It's also all we ever have. The past is gone, the future can rarely be imagined. All that is real is here and now. And if you're willing to pause for a moment and look around, it could be greater than you imagine.

How You Talk to Yourself

What does it sound like inside your head?

Most of us have an internal commentary chatting away as we go about our daily business. It can be judgmental: "Those pink leggings make you look like a flamingo." It can give us pep talks: "No, don't worry—your outfit is salmon and you look great!" It can muse: "I wonder if he was put off by your clothes?" It can curse: "Why are you always stuck walking behind the slowest people in the universe?" Sometimes mine sounds exactly like my mother: "Yes, she is dressed badly and so are you, darling—it's why you don't have a boyfriend. Now hurry up and get to work."

This inner voice differs for each of us. (I hope no one else has the dubious pleasure of hearing my disembodied mom.) Some people think in scattered words—the subconscious fills in the rest (late—bus—twenty-five minutes—work). Pictures—or visual thinking—can sometimes dominate or even decorate the self-talk. We all have a slightly different inner landscape. Getting to know the voices in my head has been a significant part of transforming my mindscape, from something resembling a volcanic Mordor to more of a luscious and only occasionally rainy forest.

See, somewhere along the way my internal monologue turned on me. The inner coach always driving me on, asking me to do better, became a bully. This self-critic was brutal and destructive to my confidence, spitting the kind of bile that no one in real life would dare say to me.

It sounded a bit like this: "Your stomach looks massive in that—really ugly. People will be repulsed by you. Look at those stains on your teeth. You shouldn't be smoking. It's disgusting. You're disgusting. You have no self-control. Why haven't you done that project you said you'd do? You're useless. You need to do it now. You're not allowed to enjoy anything until you've done it. I bet you can't do it anyway. If you can't do this you're worth nothing."

Really charming. You can't win either—you tell yourself you can't do something, and at the same time that you have to do something. Living with this voice has at times made me defensive, irritable, and unable to relate to people well. I was walking around buried in shame half the time, tight and angry from fighting off the other half. So what was the purpose of this voice? And how could I turn the volume down?

Well, once I tuned in, I realized what was going on. As much as this inner critic made life hard for me, I'd assumed it was what motivated me. I believed that if I stopped feeding this bully with worry and attention, I would end up doing nothing and then be proved right by it; if even beating myself up didn't force me into action, then how unproductive would I be if I let it go?

In reality, I was achieving *in spite* of this self-criticism, not *because* of it. And the things I didn't want to do? I still didn't do them—whether the critic dialed up the abuse or not. All that happened was that I felt much worse about them, making myself feel bad. What's the point in that? It was clear that I needed a different way of motivating myself.

At some point I gave this voice a name and character: Mr. Peanut—an unbelievable perfectionist. Naming him something silly helped a lot. Sometimes I give him a Scooby Doo–style voice too. It's hard to take a cartoon dog seriously. Doing this helped distance the critic from me as a person—and it gave me a bit of breathing room to be a human being, and do what I want sometimes, instead of constantly being nagged about what I should do.

After a while, I started to hear another quiet voice that came in response to Mr. Peanut. This new voice told me that I could do this, that I was brilliant, that I did have the ability and I would get there in the end. It ended up being much more worthwhile for me to tune into that voice (I've called her Angelica, because she's an absolute godsend) and motivate myself lovingly forward.

Even if you aren't convinced you'd succeed without your inner critic, let me put it this way: If you aren't getting where you want to go in a way that feels good, what's the point? Yes, you might end up changing your circumstances to something apparently richer, better looking, or cleverer—and you might complete that project in record time. My guess, however, is that your success will feel pretty hollow if you've had to flagellate yourself into the ground to get there, hating every minute of it. You can't hate your way into a life that feels good. Trust me, I've tried.

This life is harsh enough without you turning on your own sweet self too. There are enough battles worth fighting in this world—waging war on yourself is not one of them. Someone will let you know if you've f★★ked up, I promise you.

That leads me to the second reason I put up with Mr. Peanut for so long: protection from all those real-life critics. Somewhere deep down, I had this idea that if I could be really mean to myself, then no one would be able to hurt me, because I'd gotten there first. If I could just preempt everything bad about myself, I could toughen myself up, or I could change it or hide it before anyone noticed; then I would be safe. This just wasn't true. It actually stopped me from seeing the more immature parts of myself that needed attention.

The less savory sides of yourself won't come out into the light if your internal landscape is so full of judgment and shame—it's too painful to confront them. Your inner critic just ends up weakening your self-worth to such a low level that you can't cope with hearing or seeing anything else about yourself that might need attention—either from outside or inside. You can end up living a life in retreat—from yourself and the world, all because it's gotten thorny in your own head.

Adjusting your inner voice is a process. When I'm making lots of changes in my life or doing something new, this voice of self-doubt sometimes shows up again. I think it's just a side of me that gets scared and wants me to shrink back into a place that's more comfortable. Now I speak to my inner voice and say, "I know you're just trying to protect me, but actually I've got this." Other times I just say, "F★★k off, will you? I'm sick of you crowding my brain!"

Some days I wake up and feel so bad I think, "Wow, it's going to be pretty easy to beat myself up today." On those days, I make a vow—I say I won't tell myself a single bad thing about myself. It's surprisingly difficult. By the way, this doesn't mean being completely unselfconscious or, to use a well-worn phrase, "blowing smoke up your ass"; it means committing to reframing situations in a way that serves you and whatever you're trying to do better.

Reframe It

Once upon a time I was a manager. I found myself in a difficult work situation where I kept telling myself I'd done something wrong. Despite doing everything I possibly could, the voice telling me I wasn't good enough kept worrying away. I was running this script (or rather a script was running me) that I couldn't make my team happy and this meant I was a bad manager, they hated me, I was a terrible person, etc., etc. In the end I nixed it by telling myself, "I am glad I care enough that I keep worrying about this, even though I've done everything I can." That made the clouds clear in my brain a little.

Answering Your Inner Critic

Half of working with your inner critic is developing a louder voice to answer it—one that is kind and forgiving. You can see the emergence of your critic as a chance to creatively turn that voice around and cultivate a new voice. You can do this by consciously reframing what you're telling yourself in a positive way. For example, "I'm too aggressive and masculine" becomes "Sometimes I come across as defensive, but that's because I'm excitable and really want things to go well." Or, "My belly is fat and disgusting" becomes "I may want to lose weight, but right now I choose to love my soft, enveloping tummy, like a vintage goddess." Keep on looking for the good side of the thing you are criticizing yourself for—and it gets easier and easier to find.

Note: Be careful that once you identify the voice, you don't beat yourself up about beating yourself up—or beat yourself up about beating yourself up about beating yourself up. Mr. Peanut is clever that way—he tries to make me feel bad about feeling bad.

Your Self-Talk Transformation

Stand in the mirror—face yourself—and find things to love. Put one hand on your heart and one on your belly to comfort yourself as you do this.

The most wonderful thing I've discovered about developing a really kind inner voice is that it can't help but come into play when I speak with other people now. It's as if by developing this new compassionate way of relating to myself, suddenly I'm relating to other people in a much more understanding manner too. That in itself then reaps its own rewards when they beam love back at me. There's a phrase, "Point one finger at someone else and three fingers come pointing back at you." Now, when I hear people spouting bile at others, I feel bad for them, knowing that if it sounds that nasty externally, it must sound really mean for them in their minds. Turning this on its head, giving yourself a hug means you can share three more hugs with others.

The challenge really begins when you make a mistake. When you've done something wrong and someone else suggests you're worth less because of it. This is where I choose to separate what I've done from who I am as a person. I tell myself that even though I f★★ked up, I am not a f★★k-up. That thing I did or didn't do might have been bad, but I am not bad. And then, because I want to improve, I look objectively at why I did what I did, what I could have done, and how I could prevent it from happening again. This bettering process is a lot easier to do if every mistake you make doesn't mean you *are* a mistake. Facing up to things you've done wrong is a question of changing the behavior, rather than having to make some fundamental change to yourself.

Whenever mistakes mean that you put your actual self under threat, you begin to clam up, you get defensive, because looking at what happened, or admitting you did something wrong, means putting your entire being—who you are—on the line. The truth is, you don't need to fix yourself, because you're not broken. But you may need to fix some behavior and clean up any mess you made because of that behavior. Looking at things this way empowers you to take charge of your own destiny. Making mistakes becomes a way to make progress rather than "proof" that your inner critic was right all along.

Feelings

Emotions get a bad rap. We say a coworker is "sensitive" and wrinkle our noses, as if having feelings is the least desirable thing in the world.

When I ask my coaching clients, "How do you feel today?," often they'll struggle to reply with anything beyond "good" or "stressed." Using our feeling sense is so unfamiliar, we can barely identify our own emotions anymore. One bold gentleman simply refused to answer the question at all, telling me, "To be honest, I find emotions a bit wishy-washy."

I'm British; I get it. But this demonization of feelings does no one any good in the long term. Feelings themselves do not cause harm—it's how we respond to them that creates such chaos. When we say we are "too emotional"—we mean we don't like the way we react to having certain feelings.

> There's a word for good stress—it was coined by Hungarian endocrinologist (hormone scientist) Hans Selye—"eustress" (good), as opposed to "distress" (bad). There isn't an external difference between good and bad stress; it totally depends on, and is delineated by, our response.

It's no surprise that so many of us struggle with our reactions to emotions. We are taught to reduce them from a young age: They are dangerous; other people don't like us if we show them. One of the first things we say to a weeping child is "don't cry." We get very little chance to practice how to feel well, to hold that emotional energy in our body or release it and direct it wisely.

And so we grow up, numbing and avoiding where we can (bottle of Prosecco after work, anyone?). But suppressing emotions wastes time and energy. It's a bit like pushing a beach ball underwater. Despite a lot of exertion, it inevitably pops up anyway, exploding out of the water with force.

You can't banish emotions. Feelings are part of being human, hardwired into us for survival. Big, powerful emotions (fear, jealousy, anger, and even love) will arise in spite of our best efforts.

After a lifetime of anesthesia, experiencing that much energy is overwhelming. Our society is not set up to support or even tolerate these extreme feelings either. Much of the time we aren't allowed to share or show them in a stable environment—these emotions are actually taboo.

It's why, when something like anger comes up, we try to get rid of that energy as quickly as possible. We're in such a rush, we're so uncomfortable, we don't always expel it in useful ways. And that's when people get punched in the face.

When someone labels us "emotional," what they are really saying is: "I have no idea how to handle my own emotions, let alone yours. Seeing your emotions reminds me of this, and it is making me so uncomfortable that I am going to need to blame you for it. It is not personal; it is just that I have no template for interpreting this bodily sensation. I'm not sure what to do, and I don't like that. Therefore, right now, I will call you bad."

I'm not saying you need to go around sharing your feelings with everyone you meet, but you sure as hell need to share them with yourself. Oh, and here's another thing: Contrary to popular opinion, facing your own emotions and allowing yourself to feel them takes real courage. Anyone who says otherwise is speaking from just one emotion—and that's fear.

I'm not going to lie—emotions can be painful. That's actually okay. It's called growth. Yeah, I know it feels like sh★t. You'll survive though. The truth is, if you don't ever feel f★★ked up, you're probably doing life wrong.

Intense turmoil aside, there are actually some incredible benefits to cultivating feelings. But first, how to feel without knocking yourself (or someone else) out.

How to Feel

One way that emotions show up is as sensations in the body—they each have their own telltale footprint and feel a little different for every one of us.

Happiness might show up as a light, expansive feeling in the chest, a relaxation of the skin on the face. Disgust might appear as a sickness in the stomach, a hunching and tenseness in the shoulders. Peaceful might feel like a fanning release across the shoulders, the corners of your mouth turned up, a spacious feeling in your forehead.

It's useful to be able to identify emotions like this. Sensing in this way takes you out of your jumble of thoughts—out of your head and back into your body. Big, "scary" emotions are reduced to a collection of physical sensations—which for me always feels far more manageable. It serves as a reminder that I am not my emotions—they shift and move and change.

> There's actually no scientific consensus on the definition of emotion. The etymological root of the word emotion is from Latin—"to move out." The word "feeling" comes from the Old English "felan": to touch or have a sensory experience of; perceive, sense (something).

Separate the Thought from the Feeling

Focusing on the actual sensations occurring in your body, while noticing whether you have a preference for them or not, allows you to experience whatever you are feeling without getting caught up in a thousand different thoughts.

These thoughts often complicate and prolong the emotional experience—one negative thought sparking another negative thought, until the original thing we felt hurt or sad about suddenly appears much worse than it is. Ever had that experience where you begin crying, say, about breaking up with someone—and then you start remembering every other past failed relationship and then you begin connecting all the dots and make a little story for yourself about how you're totally unlovable—and maybe even your parents don't love you—and begin weeping harder and harder? Or you get fired from a job that you didn't want anyway, and then you start thinking you're never going to make any money, and didn't your seventh-grade teacher tell you that—and then before you know it, your problem isn't that you don't have a job but that you're worthless? Well, this method of locating and focusing on the sensations avoids going into that kind of experience.

You Can't Rationalize Your Way Out of a Storm

Separating our emotion from our thought is important because most of the time, we feel a feeling and it's strong and the next step is that we try to rationalize it. It's natural, but it's not helpful.

When you try to rationalize it away and it doesn't work, it simply makes you feel like an irrational idiot. Now, not only do you feel bad, you also feel bad about feeling bad.

The other way is even worse: We rationalize our strong feeling by exaggerating the awfulness of the situation to match the depth of our emotional response. Focusing on the physical sensation is a neutral way of going into the feeling, while still allowing its release.

Experiencing strong emotions is sometimes like being caught in the eye of a storm. And if you're caught in a storm, you don't try to get out of it; you go somewhere safe and ride it out. You can work out what to do later. Have you ever tried to give advice to someone who was having an intense emotional experience? Can they hear it? No. They get annoyed. Don't do it to yourself. Just allow the emotions to come.

Facing It, Locating It, Asking It, Loving It

Here's something you can do alone or with a friend you trust. If you're doing it solo, either write it down, speak it out loud, or record it on your phone.

★ Set a timer. Commit to fifteen minutes. This allows you to sink into your emotions, without feeling that they are overwhelming and endless.

★ Take two deep breaths, in through the nose and out through the mouth. Start asking yourself the following questions.

★ **Question 1:** "How are you feeling right now?"

★ Example answer: "I am feeling angry."

★ Response: "Thank you." Give yourself permission to feel this.

Watch out for thoughts disguised as feelings; these often come with a "like." For example, "I feel like I want to punch my boss." Remember, stress is not a feeling—it's a reaction to a feeling, or a mixture of feelings.

Tip: If you're struggling or can only come up with "I feel exhausted," change Question 1 to "What feeling are you resisting?"

★ **Question 2:** "Where do you feel this in your body?"
★ Example answers: "Contraction in my stomach" or "Heat in my face."
★ Response: "Thank you."
  Take a moment. Breathe into the sensations.

★ **Question 3:** "What does this emotion want to show you?"
★ Example answers: "That one of my boundaries has been crossed" or "It has brought up a memory."
★ Track the feeling back—what triggered it?

★ **Question 4:** "What is this emotion asking for?"
  With love, attend to your feeling and ask what it needs. Maybe you need to cry or be hugged. If one of your boundaries has been crossed, you might thank your emotion for letting you know and pledge not to allow that to happen again.
★ Now give yourself permission to let the feeling go. Say, "I am letting you go now."
★ Visualize this feeling leaving your body, as though it is a cloud heading back up to the sky. If you want, you can even open a window and "hand" the energy back to the universe.

For Me, Not to Me

The next time you're under emotional pressure, ask yourself, "How is this happening for me, rather than to me?" Imagine someone has engineered this exact configuration of events to show you something or let you learn something. What is the opportunity here for you to grow and be more powerful?

Truly Sensational

Certain emotions are physiologically very similar. Fear and excitement, for example. There's a wonderful experiment described in Ian Robertson's book *The Stress Test* where, halfway across a high, rickety suspension bridge over a deep canyon, men were stopped by a female research assistant and asked to take part in a study on the effects of scenic attractions on creativity—and, if they could, write a short story.[4] The same exercise was repeated, with the same assistant, but this time on a sturdy bridge. The men who did the exercise on the rickety bridge wrote stories full of sexual imagery and were far more likely to try to contact the research assistant personally afterward.

The explanation? The men on the bridge were already experiencing the kind of sensations prompted by risk and fear—sweaty palms, increased heart rate—when the pretty research assistant approached them. Some of the men misinterpreted the emotional signals prompted by the height of the bridge as arousal, given the presence of the female assistant. This was not the case for those men who took the test on the sturdier platform.

We can actually use this to our advantage sometimes. If you can interpret anxiety as excitement—as being ready to go—because the physiological symptoms are so similar. It may actually change how you think and feel about the situation, enabling you to make better choices and take bolder action.

This phenomenon also lies behind one of the major benefits of allowing yourself to feel. So many challenging emotions share overlapping sensations with pleasant emotions. You can't numb one emotion without numbing a range of emotions. If you start allowing yourself to feel, you might have a more acute experience of grief, sadness, disappointment—but you'll also be able to feel more happiness, joy, contentment, and love. It might sometimes be uncomfortable and messy— but messy beautiful.

Emotions Are Your "Sherpa"

Some people have an idea of what they think will make them happy—the ideal body shape, the good job, the hefty salary, the nice car, the big house, the romantic relationship. Happiness has taken on a certain form for those people, and they look to achieve those things as their route to it. Actually, most of the time the form is irrelevant—it's the feeling underneath the form that's important: the self-worth, the satisfaction, the intimacy, the feeling of being valued, the love, the sex, the freedom. You can work your way into the grave getting all of the things in the "form" list and still be utterly miserable. Because those weren't the things you actually wanted—it was the feeling you thought they would provide you with that you craved.

This is important when it comes to feelings, because when you learn to be guided by your emotions, you can start making decisions based on what feels good instead of what looks or sounds good, or even what "rationally" makes sense. If your thoughts are saying one thing and your emotions and body another, you can bet the latter is more truthful. In those situations, it's worth tuning in, and asking why—and what—a certain thing is giving you. In this way, emotions can be thought of as "energetic information": sensations in our body that can provide important clues for us to get to know ourselves, helping guide us toward a happier life.

Storytelling

"Storytelling" has most likely been a big part of your life without you even noticing—and will probably continue that way until you die. It's a stealthy yet powerful, invisible yet omnipresent force in our lives.

Storytelling is an innately human urge—we construct narratives to share with each other on such a fundamental scale that it's as instinctual to our nature as drinking water.

From an early age, we are read stories by our parents; as babies we are bewitched and soothed by the sounds of language, which, as we grow, gradually become comprehensible as bedtime stories. Teachers share instructive fables to teach us simple lessons, and, of course, we are protected by "cautionary tales," warning us of the world's perils.

Stories have many functions in our lives—we use them to empathize with different viewpoints and assimilate and absorb knowledge (show me a TED Talk that doesn't have at least one story). We use them to make sense of the world, which might be one reason why we get so frustrated when certain narratives challenge us with their meaning, or films or books fail to provide a satisfying ending.

Yet more often than not, storytelling is so instinctive to us that we aren't always conscious of when and why we do it. That's particularly the case when it comes to the stories we tell about ourselves.

Self-Scheming Storytellers

As consummate storytellers, we often edit—depending on our audience and medium. We know we do this, and quite often it's so slight and subconscious we wouldn't even call it "lying." After all, we wouldn't present the same version of our story to a potential employer as we would to a potential partner on a first date.

Underneath all of this surface storytelling are the stories we tell ourselves about ourselves. Messages from authority figures, information we receive from our parents, and our emotional memories and shared experiences converge to construct a mental narrative about our own lives, our own character, the sort of person we are, and the sort we aren't. We tell ourselves stories about who and what we like and dislike, what we are good or bad at, and how people relate to us. Psychologists call these sets of self-perceptions "self schemes." I'm going to call them stories.

I call them stories, rather than beliefs or an ethos, to emphasize that this identity-making process is drawn from a narrative we create for ourselves, a collection of stories that are fluid and far from fixed. There's no right or wrong story—there's simply helpful or unhelpful, interesting or boring. We are scriptwriters here, often unconscious ones, selecting certain events, applying a lens, stripping or saving details, positioning pivotal plot points, characterizing heroes and villains, and, most importantly, defining a certain role for ourselves.

There is nothing inherently wrong with doing this, provided your stories are healthy, flexible, and constructive—that is, they help you feel positive and allow you to get the best out of life.

The problem is, many of our own personal stories don't meet these criteria at all. They say that we've been left, let down, or victimized. They focus on being hurt, damaged, and abused. That isn't to say that any of these things didn't or won't happen, aren't painful, or should be ignored or edited out of the narrative, but if it is only these elements that are selected to play starring roles in your story—while personal power, redemption, love, community, and growth are forgotten—then you're left to play out a tragedy, with yourself as the unfortunate protagonist, fated to failure.

Why do we do this? Partly because our brains like to generalize, using the information we've received in the past to decide how to act in certain situations—what to do and useful strategies. Otherwise every time we face a situation that is only slightly different from past experiences, we'll feel totally floored.

The problem occurs when we overgeneralize, then apply a layer of confirmation bias over the top. We assume that because one person has treated us badly, or one situation turned out a certain way, all people will treat us badly and all situations will turn out that way. We use certain circumstances as "proof" of our flaws and we live this fixed narrative, going about our lives with distorted and even damning stories about ourselves and others, only heeding the data that fit these beliefs. Perhaps that's why they say first impressions count: Once we've got a story running, the brain is tempted to ignore, disbelieve, or disregard any contrary evidence. Through the power of storytelling, a bad experience becomes a belief that has the power to rule and ruin our lives.

For example, the school bully might have teased you for being overweight, and other students, also scared of the bully, might have laughed. You were very hurt by this experience, which made you feel not only overweight but also disrespected, unattractive, unloved, and worthless.

You grow up and lose weight, however you still believe that you are unattractive and unlovable because you have this story. Now, when you go on dates, every gesture, statement, joke, or question is filtered and analyzed through the lens of "they probably won't like me." Your brain becomes conditioned to this process, surveying and selecting only information that confirms this story.

You mistake someone's shy nature as lack of interest and so you don't call them back, even though you might have liked to. When a different date asks to meet up again, you assume it is from pity or boredom, so you feign disinterest and they withdraw. Left with no one, you now make your story about being unattractive true again. Convenient, eh?

Even when all the contrary evidence piles up, overwhelming the original narrative, the story still needs to be true: You finally meet someone who likes and pursues you. You end up becoming a couple, but deep down you wonder if there is something wrong with them for being with you. Eventually you sabotage the relationship, convinced it could not last anyway, because that would contradict the storyline.

Congratulations, you were right! Once again, your doubts are justified. Your story is true, because you've made it true.

Our stories can become self-fulfilling prophecies—even when they aren't ours. Your self-perception might be inherited from your mother, for example. Adding insult to injury, not only are these stories downgrading your experience of your life, they aren't even yours! Recognizing these stories is imperative, because unless you catch them at their root and tear them out, they can derail your life. It's not just about subconsciously confirming them—sometimes they control us because we are desperately fighting to disprove them, scrambling to the top of the corporate ladder because your geography teacher said you would never succeed. Developing an arrogant attitude to refute a deeply entrenched story of worthlessness. That's no good either because these old chestnuts are still there, dictating your life and your choices.

For a long time, I was so hooked on achievement (in reaction to a story that I wasn't "good enough"). No matter how many accolades I won, this story revolved in my head, stronger than the facts, which could never win against a story I had created for myself. Our brains are funny old things, electing to be right rather than happy. The soggy logic is something like this—we might be miserable, but at least we feel in control!

Five Steps to Rewriting Your Story

1. Be ready: The first step to rewriting your stories is being willing to let go of the old ones. You might not be ready yet. Often we need to feel heard, to express our emotions fully and have that validated, before we can work on moving forward. To rewrite our stories, there has to be a decision to stop defining ourselves through hurt or pain, but in order to do that, sometimes we need to delve into that pain, explore it, analyze it, and understand it rather than dodging, ignoring, or burying it any longer.

2. It can be tough to relinquish old stories, which we cling to stubbornly in fear or familiarity. At this juncture, pause. It's time to introduce acceptance. Accept that things did not go the way you wanted them to, and accept that you would have preferred a different outcome to the situation. Accept things you were not okay with, and that not being okay with them is acceptable. Accepting these disappointments can resolve the conflict you feel toward them, removing emotional clutter and freeing up space so that you can reframe the circumstances differently moving forward.

3. Identify an old or unhelpful story: Look for a place in your life where you feel stuck—where you keep repeating the same behavior, which is not giving you the result you desire. Or maybe look at a part of your life that makes you feel out of control and powerless to change it. Identify something that has happened that cannot be undone and makes you think that now "your life is terrible," or you feel someone has "done" something to you. These are indicators that a story is twisting your thoughts or actions and that a rewrite of your narrative would benefit you.

4. Flesh out the narrative: Let's use being cheated on by an ex-partner as an example. It's a situation that lots of people have been in, and it can feel very painful when it happens to you. It doesn't necessarily have to be, though—at least not forever. Get a pen and paper for this. It's hard to work with our thoughts when they feel like impenetrable clouds of amorphous negativity. What you aim to create is a neutral description of what happened (challenge yourself to describe the event or situation in the most skeletal way possible) and then strip away every possible meaning. For example, "A person I had agreed to be in a monogamous relationship with slept with someone else without telling me first."

5. Conclusions: What did you extrapolate from this situation? What were you telling yourself at that time? Example: "I was hurt. I was betrayed. I couldn't understand why he hadn't told me. I wasn't enough. I didn't understand why I didn't see it coming. I wasn't able to protect myself. I couldn't trust anyone again.

I couldn't trust myself. Relationships weren't safe. People aren't to be trusted."

6. Rewrite the story: There are several ways to go about this—different questions and methods will resonate for different people with different stories. Often, there'll be a light bulb moment, almost like when you look at those optical illusions and you finally see the faces instead of the candlestick, or the old woman instead of the young woman. Other times it takes a bit more work. One therapist asked me, "If I went out and described your story to 100 different people, do you think they would come to the same conclusion as you?" I had to admit that they wouldn't.

The stories we have about ourselves and the world don't change overnight. Even once we accept rationally that there is the possibility of an altered version of events that might be just as true as the one we're captive to, it takes time to weave stories of growth and empowerment into our conscious experience of the world. One emotional occurrence can activate a cluster of stories, and in those situations it can be hard to weave a narrative that serves us rather than saddens us. It ultimately requires repetition and practice. Ask yourself three questions whenever you're in a place that feels bad:

★ What story am I telling myself here?
★ Is it serving me?
★ Could I tell myself anything else that would move me closer to the result I want?

The process of recognizing, accepting, and reframing harmful stories that we may have relied on to make sense of our world for a long time is a tough practice to master. The hardest part is letting go. Our brains have become so invested in these narratives and interpreted so many events to fit them that clearing away the detritus obscuring our true self can be disorienting and painful. It's confusing and humbling to realize that we're telling ourselves these hurtful things—that we are causing ourselves this pain because of the narrative we're draping all over the event.

Whenever you are tempted to abandon unraveling your stories because it's painful or difficult, imagine these stories as poison ivy wrapping itself around a tree. Left untended, the ivy's vines grow swiftly and imperceptibly, taking more than its share of light and nourishment so subtly and totally that eventually our poor tree is strangled by the creeper. In this way, accepting and feeding a negative narrative weakens us too. All that lives, thrives, and flourishes is the story, while we are left with nothing but pain.

Choose to cast yourself as a hero instead. You can defend your inner kingdom against these enemies to your well-being by realizing your story and staying vigilant to the desire to falsify "evidence" of your failings automatically. Enlist a fellow warrior to help you out—my friends call me out when I start relating some negative narrative, nudging me and saying, "Great story you've got there." Or, "Was it completely unbearable? You look like you are still here to me."

Arm yourself with acceptance and forgiveness, don your reframing lens, and tell yourself that you will overcome these mental monsters. The story isn't over yet, after all.

Your Body

We all live with a creature. A soft, forgiving but, nonetheless, perishable creature. This beautiful creature, who was born with us, is unique to us in many ways. It can look after itself most of the time, but it does ask us for certain things so that we can both live happily.

We can't exist without this creature, and yet many of us forget it or disrespect it, even though this soft animal has our best interests at heart. We treat our creature like an inconvenience, we ignore it until it cries out for attention, and even then we pretend to hear something different.

This creature is our body. We live in a culture that is mean to our creature selves in many ways. That rates it only for what it looks like or what it can do compared to other people. Yet this creature has its own form of wisdom that can't be argued with. It is worth listening to. After all, we don't just live with a creature, we live inside a creature. It's important for us to learn how to work with our creature self if we want to live well and do great things.

Sometimes, it's not a mystery why we feel the way we do when we actually take note of how we treat our bodies. I once went to a therapist for anxiety and insomnia. I was in a bad way—close to falling apart really. I told her all about my failed relationships, how I couldn't make friends. I branched into a long story about how I was in the wrong job and everyone hated me, and I was pretty sure I hated everyone too.

We also talked about my lifestyle. She asked me about my caffeine intake—how many cups of coffee I drank a day (five), and how many Diet Cokes (three). She asked me what time I went to bed (10 p.m.) and what time I put my phone away (midnight). She asked how much alcohol I drank in a week (a bottle of wine … mostly on a Friday night) and what exercise I took (does getting public transport count?). She took note of how long I spent in front of my computer screen (eleven hours a day) and what I did in my leisure time (dating is a legitimate hobby, right?).

As we took this inventory, it became increasingly clear to me that a psychology degree was not necessary to solve at least part of my problem. The way I was living—well, I wouldn't treat a dog that way. Quite the opposite. If I saw a dog owner do this I would be ranting about the rightness of owning animals when it's clear you can't take care of them. Yet in that we all have bodies, we all have our own animal—and we frequently abuse it.

A teacher at the organization where I trained to be a coach once asked me a question that really made me wake up to this. We were talking about how hard I worked and how tired I was and how I was just refusing to slow down. Then she asked me: "Do you really want to be here? On this planet?"

It made me realize my body was more than just a fleshy structure for carting my head around—that my physical self had needs and desires. If I wanted to be on this planet, I needed to stop ignoring the messages my body was giving me.

Every creature has different needs and preferences, and the first step is getting to know what our body likes and dislikes. When it comes to your own body, I'm a big believer that though it's good to also listen to experts, deep down you know your body best. That became especially obvious to me when I got ill.

I had chronic fatigue syndrome (ME) for the better part of ten years, beginning at age thirteen. Doctors don't really understand what causes this illness, which, along with extreme tiredness, comes with delectable symptoms such as fierce muscle pain, sore throats, dizziness, and headaches. They aren't sure what makes some people recover either. The severity of the symptoms changes from day to day, but, in my case, at my worst I couldn't walk. My body felt so heavy and I felt so weak that I could only crawl to the toilet. Things got worse before they got better. It wasn't clear I would ever recover. It was rotten.

> The atoms that make up our body are mostly empty space. If we lost all our empty atomic space, we would fit into a cube less than $\frac{1}{500}$ of a centimeter on each side.[5]

I did learn a few things, though. Such as that there's nothing like having a "mysterious" illness if you want 1,000 contradictory pieces of advice propelled your way. Some people suggested I should sleep more; some said I was probably sleeping too much. Other people told me I should exercise (but ... I can't walk!). Meanwhile, some suggested total bed rest. Or that total bed rest wasn't enough and that I must completely rest my mind and not look or listen to a single thing. That I should change what I'm eating, that I should quit sugar, or dairy, or wheat or only eat raw food. I should take this tonic twice daily or drink Chinese herbal tea. That I had an allergy to electricity, or wool, or water. That I needed antidepressants.

And then if I did those things and none of them worked, I was definitely faking it. Sometimes I felt like actually being ill was only half the problem—the other half was managing people's reactions to it.

In the end, I made a slow recovery by continually doing what felt possible and fun. My granny moved in to look after me; we both wanted to move slowly but still find enjoyment in the little things, like a short walk and ice cream by the canal. It took me a long while from that point to getting back to school, and then it was a struggle from there not to beat myself up over all the things I could no longer do. I still get flare-ups from time to time.

I'm not a doctor, and I'm not telling you what to do. What I might suggest is that you check in with yourself, and see if your creature is happy with what you are doing now. Reflect on this without shame or judgment. Swap any "shoulds" for "coulds." When we say we "should" do something, it feels tight and punishing. Saying "could" instead opens us up to possibility. Try it.

Once you find what feels good for you, think about making those choices a practice. Mark the space in your planner to exercise, rest, cuddle, or get outside as "sacred time"— nonnegotiable slots in your day or week that you use to nourish yourself.

Commit to doing these "sacred time" things regularly, even when your mind is tempted to resist or it becomes inconvenient, as a way of attending to your creature self.

This is a process. Calling it a practice signals to yourself that it is not a quick hit and it's okay if you don't get it right straight away. We are relearning how to love our creature selves. It doesn't happen overnight.

It's worth continuing to practice because we learn new ways of thinking and behaving through repetition. Choice plus action, over and over again, is the way we make lasting changes in our lives.

Give yourself a score out of ten at the end of each section about how satisfied you are with this particular area of your life—this will give you clarity on where you might want to focus your attention first.

Movement

You can tell me you don't enjoy exercise, but don't tell me you don't enjoy movement. You *are* movement. Every cell of your body engages in activity every second of the day. We are all constantly in motion; it's the essence of who we are. When we stop moving, we die.

Movement is how we engage with the world; it's bodily expression. Physicality is one of the cornerstones of living.

This epiphany finally made me embrace exercise.

That's right—being barked at by a sports teacher at the bottom of a gym rope didn't work, and being told I wasn't "beach body–ready" just made me feel angry. Gyms were smelly, noisy vanity closets, and team sports were just another way of feeling left out.

I bypassed the emotional landmine that is the exercise industry and instead viewed movement as my birthright as the owner of a body. To bastardize an oft-attributed-to-Socrates quote, I told myself I would not grow old without seeing the beauty and strength of which my body was capable. It's not always easy, especially if you have a physical disability, but part of being human is working with what we have, day after day, to reach the most that is available to us.

It isn't about being "good" at basketball or the best at tennis; it is just about enjoying how your body moves, in any way that feels good.

And *voilà*! Exercise became fun. I rediscovered the joy that lay latent in my body when I started to make time for moving as expression rather than another obligation to fail at.

I dance, and I love the way no limb is left behind as you tell emotional stories with your body. The mental challenge of learning new moves means there is no space for anything but focus and joy.

I practice yoga every day. I like its goalless nature—every stretch is valued for its own unique place in your journey. I love that I keep discovering new muscles and that my body begins to lengthen—and change shape—just as I breathe and relax into a position.

Exercise that gets my heart rate up has been an important part of strengthening my creature too. When I first started coaching, I was working from home, and while I loved helping people, my body and mind felt heavy from the depth of the emotional service required daily. Yoga wasn't enough—I needed something faster to metabolize all those feelings running through me. That's the beauty of movement; if emotions are energetic information, then, for me, moving quickly is energetic processing of that download.

Although I didn't begin consciously exercising as a way to challenge myself, it's something I've begun to lean into. A kind of alchemy happens in the mind when you practice strength and capability exercises. You might be training to make your legs stronger, but somehow you personally feel stronger too. More powerful in your mind, stronger as a human, more capable to handle the curveballs that life throws at you. As I face the challenge of running that last mile against the wind and continually survive, I'm encouraged to take on challenges off the track too. It probably helps that, when I run, I think of myself as Wonder Woman, in training to be a superhero.

Getting Started

Even aspiring superheroes struggle to get out of bed sometimes. Fortunately, your body is incredibly adaptive and gets better at whatever you choose to do with it. Unfortunately, I had been training my body to sit down for eleven hours a day for the past decade. I didn't even think about beginning to exercise until the pain started.

After holding myself tightly at my desk for one day too many, my shoulders began screaming when I turned too fast, my neck seared with heat, and I swear I could hear my wrists squeaking. I couldn't type on my phone for too long without feeling like my hand had morphed into painful concrete. I'd gotten so good at being sedentary, my body was seizing up.

Knowing I needed to move, though, still wasn't enough for me to actually begin exercising. It was about clearing the blocks that were stopping me from doing it, as well as dangling some short-term carrots to get over that initial hurdle.

If you're struggling to move more, I hope that sharing what stopped me and how I got over it will give you some ideas.

"I Don't Have Time"

First of all, is this really true? Because I actually did have time, but my mind threw this up as a real reason, when it was just an excuse. I was also trying to justify why I hadn't done it before, because I was a bit ashamed.

How I got over this: I hate gyms, so I bought new running shoes and a backpack and kept them at work so I could jog at lunchtime or part of the way home. In this way, I actually felt like I was being very productive, by commuting and exercising all in one shot—or using my break well: It wasn't like I had to "manufacture" an extra slot in the day.

"I Can't Be Bothered"

It can be hard to find the motivation. It can feel tedious. I know—it's how I felt too.

How I got over this: I told myself "Just do it for fifteen minutes—you can stop at any time after that." Turns out that, after fifteen minutes, I began to enjoy it. There are loads of fifteen-minute exercise classes on YouTube too.

The other thing that helped is getting people to hold me (somewhat) accountable—finding people who wanted to do thirty-day challenges with me on YouTube. There's a January thirty-day yoga challenge with a new video every day, and I wanted to do all of them to catch up. See if you can set yourself a challenge and find yourself an accountability buddy.

"It's Boring"

It *was* boring. I was used to the speed of breaking-news headlines, my thoughts moving superfast on adrenaline. In comparison, my body felt slow and heavy and clunky, and, frankly, I felt no good at it.

How I got over this: Instead of going for coffee, I would go for a class or a walk with someone. I told myself that my response to the thought of exercise here was just showing me the state of my mind—it's so busy it can't switch off to work at a different speed. I used reverse psychology, saying to myself that the less I was enjoying this, the more I really needed this. I also looked for things I *did* find fun—like dancing.

"I'm Too Tired—I Should Rest"

Here's where you need a bit of love to soothe your reluctance. Whenever I felt like this, I would treat myself—and not with food. I'd use these treats as actions—as kind, pleasurable rituals to ease myself into whatever I was resisting. For yoga, I would first draw the curtains and light lots of candles. I bought a new "exercise" perfume to pep me up for the gym and shift my mental space. For dance, I'd allow myself to spend money on a class—or I'd buy new socks for running. I'd remind myself that it was my mind that was tired, or overstimulated, not my body.

"I Feel Fat"

Yes, every time I chose to exercise, I had to face my body. Or rather, I had to face my feelings about my body. (This was when I realized I not only had shame over my weight, but I had shame over feeling less than body-positive too. Ah, judging my own judgment, the shame about shame. My favorite style of self-indulgence.)

My tired, thick body made me feel as though moving it was pointless—that I'd never lose weight or get fit. I'd get this heavy feeling in my stomach, which felt like it was telling me, "Why bother?"

How I got over this: There's no magic button for this one. The more I sat with these feelings and thoughts, the more I got used to them, and the less uncomfortable they became— a bit like exercise. I reminded myself that choosing to move was in itself an act of self-care, which made moving less about weight loss and more about the experience itself—and I focused on how I could do this gracefully, training myself to trust that moving was good for me. I thanked my body that it could move, for holding me up, or for giving me endorphins.

How could you solve this problem? Get creative—and loosen the purse strings a little if you can afford it. What do you spend on things that don't benefit your body?

If, like me, you don't think the excuses your brain is giving you are the real reason you're resisting exercise, get a friend you trust to help you. All they need to do is ask the following questions and thank you for each answer you give:

1. "What's stopping you from exercising?"
2. "What's underneath that?"
3. "What are you resisting?"

Let them repeatedly ask until they feel they have a true answer—maybe set a timer for five or ten minutes. Then, when you have a list of five or more things, brainstorm with them to give you other ideas for getting over this hump.

Rest

It's been over 300 years since Isaac Newton said that what goes up must come down and almost definitely didn't get hit on the head by an apple.

It's fun to be up and active, and sometimes it does feel like we have a lot to do, but we all need to come down. The trick, I've learned, is to plan rest periods, because quite often we aren't so good at taking rest, even when it's needed. How familiar do phrases like this sound? "I won't take a lunch break—I don't have the time." "Yoga makes me sleepy … it's too boring." Another one I sometimes hear is: "I won't sit down, or I'll never get up again."

Hey! Slowing down only feels uncomfortable when we're going way too fast. Yoga isn't making you sleepy; you're goddamn exhausted! And sit down, or your body will force you to sit down. Everything can wait while you take a break and live. Promise. The truth is that the more jarring it feels to slow down, the greater the difference between stillness and the pace you were going, and the more your body and mind need to pause.

I like this story about Mahatma Gandhi, who, when told by his advisors that he had a busy day ahead and might need to skip his morning meditation, said that he must actually meditate for two hours instead of one. For twice as much work, twice as much space and clarity are needed.

We think we go fast because we have so much to do and it's the only way to get it all done. That's nonsense. Slow your mind down and slow your body down, and the things you don't need to worry about will drop away of their own accord. Our vision clears up when we slow down— we can't see what's necessary when we're running at high speed. On top of that, we can then actually attend to the things that are important with the attention they deserve. That includes the people we care about, whose feelings get trampled on when we are flying by the seat of our pants from one frenetic activity to another. Going too fast makes us impatient and irritable with the ones we love, and in turn we can either internalize that frustration with ourselves for not being compassionate or seek to further disconnect from anyone or anything that might get in our way, which leads to isolation. It's not an honorable way to live, but we all find ourselves there at times. I use my irritability as the canary in the coal mine; the more it flares up, the more I know I need to slow things down.

We aren't used to this. People mistake speed for efficiency, confuse stress with self-importance, and substitute busyness for meaning.

Too many of us live our lives at a manufactured speed, with everything whizzing past us at 100 miles per hour. Fueled by adrenaline, we can hardly see what's going on around us accurately, let alone feel or make decisions well. On one level we know we are going too fast. We layer sensation on top of sensation, activity on top of activity, sugar on top of caffeine. Anything to avoid feeling the deep fatigue, the tension, the sadness that's building up in our bodies. Then our scheduled vacation arrives and we get a horrific cold, or we take a few deep breaths and burst into tears.

Unwind Well

We all get busy and lost in our own heads, but we don't need to stay there. It's much better to unwind a little bit at a time and naturally—to come down from busyness deliberately, rather than wait until your body crashes and bed rest is inconveniently forced upon you.

The question you want to ask yourself is "How do I like to relax?" If you don't know, get curious. Active ways of resting might be things like reading a book, going for a walk, taking a yoga class, calling your grandma—even cleaning or cooking. See if you can think of five right now. Passive ones might be having a salt bath, a cuddle, a massage. Maybe watching a Disney movie. Experiment with what feels good.

Change the way you think about rest—not as inactivity but rather as developing the skill of slowing down. Sports coaches schedule strict rest days for their athletes; it's a vital part of their training. You want to be able to change gears—not have only one speed you can operate at.

It's hard to prioritize rest, because modern society doesn't seem to value relaxation. But even fields have fallow years—in which, deliberately, nothing is planted—to give the soil a chance to revitalize itself.

This is ancient wisdom. Contrary to popular thought, rest is how you grow stronger. It's regeneration. Every culture has a rest day—it's been like that since time began.

The most loving thing you can do for yourself, at any moment, is slow. it. right. down. Stop. Take a deep breath. Soften your jaw. Allow your belly to expand. Let your shoulders sink down. Allow the skin on your face to release. This is a pace that is more caring for you, for your body, and for whatever it is you are attending to. Look how much easier it is to feel and see life when you're in this softer spot.

> Parkinson's law is the adage that work expands to fill the time available to complete it. It was invented by a civil servant in the 1950s, who had observed it in practice during his time working in government.[6]

Sometimes, people come to me for coaching, and they say, "I need help managing my time." They turn up for their sessions every week, and they seem to have accomplished a lot in their lives. They really don't have a time management problem; they have an "overwhelm" problem, they have a self-love problem, and they have a trust problem. I empathize. I think I was going so fast at one point in my life that I could have made being a meditation teacher stressful. Sometimes the thoughts were popping in my head so fast that I could barely get the words out.

So I understand when I hear clients say, "Basically, I need three of me." I tell them, "Oh yes, and what if I gave you three of you? You'd be back here next week, saying, 'I think I actually need six of me.'" The problem is never that there's not enough of you; it's that you think you are not enough, and one symptom of that pain is that you're trying to do too much.

When you slow down, regardless of the number of things you have to do, you tell yourself, "I want to enjoy life." That life is important and you are important. If you only had one slice of a delicious dessert, you would savor it, taking each bite slowly and deliberately and with relish. Why wouldn't you do the same with life? Cramming your life with piles of nonsense just makes it feel shorter.

Good things feel better stretched out. Feelings can breathe given airtime. Time dilutes pain too. Everyone wins when we slow. it. right. down. With space, the unimportant drops off, inviting in clarity and creating more room. And more often than not, it's love that rushes into those gaps, something we could all use more of.

Try making it your mission to include a half-hour of nothing in your schedule every day. Put it in before everything else.

Drinking, Smoking, Drugs

First things first, and this might be a shocker, but whatever you are doing, it's okay. If you're drinking too much, smoking too much, or taking too many drugs, that's okay. It might not be healthy, and it might not even be legal, but I'm not a doctor, police officer, or judge, and from where I'm sitting, in my human skin, with my human mind, you're not a *bad* person.

That's not quite all I have to say on the issue, though, because let's face it, smoking is a terrible ROI ("Yes, I will pay money to endure a slow death and smell terrible"). Meanwhile, alcohol is attractively packaged poison, and illegal drugs are a shortcut to having a whole host of totally chaotic situations and people showing up in your life.

So why say it's okay? Well, I heartily approve of whatever situation you find yourself in with drink, drugs, or smoking because you're here now, and shaming or admonishing you won't solve anything. You already know all the things about why you shouldn't do it. And guess what. You do them anyway. So let's not go down that dead end of schoolteacher righteousness. I do and have done some of the bad things too. Telling myself off (or someone else telling me off) just makes me feel stressed out, which in turn makes me want to seek the crutch I was being told off about in the first place.

The thing is, if you're using substances, smoking, or drinking, you probably have really legitimate reasons for doing the things you're doing. I'm guessing it's more than just "this feels temporarily good" too. You might be smoking because you enjoy the connection or the break you get outside. You might be drinking because you find it difficult to relax.

You might have some feelings that you're not sure how to work with. Maybe the people you're hanging out with have that problem, and you're just going along with it because you want to feel part of something. It could be that there are situations you feel particularly uncomfortable in and you don't know how to manage that. It could be that life just feels a bit sucky, and why not check out and care about nothing for a while?

This might not be a full-blown addiction, where it's about to take over your life, but it's still an unhealthy way to relate to your emotions, even if it's "letting off steam" with six beers on a Friday.

Think about whether you want to continue down that path. Because it might be fun occasionally, but it's not the best use of body, mind, time, or money. Plus, you might have been drinking, smoking, or taking drugs to help you avoid or "numb" a particular issue or feeling, and unless everything has magically changed, including your thinking, well, you're just going to need more and more to help you cope. It doesn't really solve the issue; it's just temporary relief. The drinking, smoking, or drugs is just a Band-Aid. There's only so long it will work for you. If, indeed, it works at all.

Addiction

More frustrating than all of that, at least for me, is that these substances, which you may have originally used to let go and feel more free, actually end up putting more constraints on you.

Your choices get hijacked by a bunch of toxins because, biologically and psychologically, it becomes harder and harder to turn them down. The reason you first said yes to the wine, the cigarette, or the joint is not the reason you are going to keep saying yes. And at some point the reason you say "yes" will end up being because you don't feel you can say "no."

You can.

It's just hard.

The reasons we do these things are complicated and we even hide them from ourselves. We didn't want to confront them in the first place, which is why we started drinking/smoking/taking drugs. Unfortunately, the original issue will not magically disappear once you stop doing the thing either. You'll still need a way to handle the whatever-was-troubling-you in the first place.

There's always a reason you are doing what you are doing, or started doing what you are doing, and it's worth investigating this, ideally with a therapist. Then, when you find out what the unhealthy activity gives you, you can find out a way to replicate that without the substance.

Perhaps you'll find that if you're a little less punishing with yourself, you don't need to drink as much. Or if you schedule something with a sober friend, they can help you keep on track during a time when you know you like to drink (maybe after a stressful day). Find an activity you like, that relaxes you or is fun, or that even gives you a high—that is healthy and doesn't involve the substance. It might involve making some new friends.

This is not medical advice, and I am not an addiction expert. I heartily endorse enrolling in a twelve-step program if any of these substances have appeared or are appearing in your life in a way that feels hard to handle. Notice that I don't limit this to whether or not you're the individual actually doing the consuming—because that's the thing about these substances: They have a large radius of influence.

> Although the biggest twelve-step program is Alcoholics Anonymous, there are also a number of lesser-known groups that follow this pattern for countering addiction—for example, Clutterers Anonymous, Underearners Anonymous, and On-Line Gamers Anonymous.

Additionally, if you have an addiction and want help, get some medical advice, because there's a wealth of knowledge and support out there for how to quit effectively. Many people have walked this path before you, so you will be well-held.

I have the utmost empathy for anyone who's struggled with addiction or substance misuse, or even if you're just someone who knows they like a certain thing a bit too much. I have addiction issues in my family, have had my own personal battles, and have met a lot of recovering addicts. They are some of the strongest, most courageous, sensitive people I know.

Using substances, even recreationally, is just a manifestation of something happening persistently inside us that wants and deserves our attention and that we're very uncomfortable with; we don't want to look at it and see what it might need. Sometimes, it's just something that needs to be felt, an emotion that needs to be released or expressed, and we don't know how to let it out—it doesn't feel socially acceptable. It might even feel unsafe. And so we seek to numb it or bury it.

We are all coping with such things. People who "use" aren't any different from the person who is excessive in their gym attendance, or the compulsive shopper, or the workaholic. Even the person who is just incredibly busy in life—busy avoiding their own feelings. We all try to avoid, repress, and numb; it's just that our methods often look different—some are healthier than others—and some are deemed less shameful.

If you take away one thing from this section, it's that I don't think addiction is anything to be ashamed of. Drugs, smoking, and drinking are not good for our bodies, though. Let's try to be a little kinder with ourselves and choose the loving thing.

Try to keep a diary of how much you drink/smoke/consume, and notice when this happens. What thoughts are going through your head? What feelings do you have?

Skin Time

We have a deep primitive need for physical touch—an aching appetite that has become so taboo in our society that we all but pretend it doesn't exist. This isn't necessarily a desire for sexual contact, though, for some, sex is the only acceptable way to get that need met.

Psychologists call it "skin hunger." Prisoners kept in solitary confinement know this peculiar starvation well. Chelsea Manning, who spent nine months isolated in this way, called it "no touch" torture.[7]

Convicted murderer Peter Collins, who died of cancer in a Canadian prison, made a film called *Fly in the Ointment* about a prolonged period in solitary confinement. In it, he described how he was so hungry for physical contact that a fly that landed on his leg excited him, and he imagined it was the touch of his wife.

"I was greedy for human touch, so I closed my eyes and pretended it was her fingers," he explained.

That experience nourished him so much that, during his time in solitary confinement, he would bite the inside of his cheek and smear the blood on his leg to attract more flies.

This is an extreme example, but, increasingly, many of us are living such isolated lives that lack of physical contact—or "skin time," as I like to call it—affects more than just prisoners. Human touch just doesn't happen as naturally as it should anymore. We are all living farther apart. One woman who follows me on Twitter, but didn't want to be named, told me:

"My good friends are all people I met through social media and we talk daily, but it's not the same. My best friend has moved away, and I'm in a long-distance relationship."

The concept of community (more on this later) as it once was is crumbling, leaving older people and those without partners or families at risk of loneliness. A friend who works as a general practitioner told me that she suspects a few elderly patients regularly come in for an examination when nothing is wrong, purely for the physical contact.

The increasingly vivid issues of sexual consent and harassment mean platonic touch, especially across genders, is a sensitive issue. When I asked across my social media networks, one man told me he deeply missed physical contact when not in a relationship but was scared to ask for a hug "in case it was taken the wrong way." He added, "I've not had anyone initiate it with me either."

In some friendship groups, it is not usual to hug, particularly man to man. One of the people in my meditation group told me that her friends hug so lightly that it just feels like a pat on the back. When she got some cats, something strange happened: "Suddenly I had this affectionate response to being touched that was so deeply nourishing. It's why changing my living circumstances and possibly moving away from my cats is a hard no."

Meanwhile, in some circles, touch is still considered "creepy" or "effeminate," leaving some men afraid to ask for this primal human need to be met for fear of being mocked or excluded.

"I'd be scared of looking gay," one man told me.

Another said he'd love to, but "I don't know how to. No one taught me. I never saw it modeled. None of my male friends did either, with rare exceptions. I'm afraid of it. Of the reaction, rejection, discomfort. I remember vividly traveling in Turkey—male platonic touch is just normal there. I was shocked. Jealous."

Touch as Therapy

I was a student at a boarding school, and when I arrived there, I volunteered to teach people with special needs how to use computers. One man who had impaired brain and motor function put his hand on my knee and didn't remove it. I realized it was the first time I'd been touched in about four weeks, as I was a bit shy with friends and I hadn't been home. It made me feel really sad.

There are still times now where I forget how much I love and need comforting, platonic touch. I was really upset once, and a friend hugged me and stroked my hair; it just felt blissfully soothing. Another time, I was sitting in my living room with a male friend having an unusually honest conversation, when he said to me, "I'd really like to give you a cuddle. Can I?" I'd been dealing with this headache that hadn't gone away all day, and as I put my head on his chest, this embarrassingly large exhale came out of me and the pain in my head just shifted. Skin hunger always creeps up on me slowly, the need I don't realize I have until it gets satiated, and then my whole body relaxes and sighs with contentment.

Touch is the first sense to develop, appearing at eight weeks after conception.

On a chemical level, supportive touch triggers hormonal changes equivalent to knocking back a well-being cocktail. Even just a hug lowers levels of cortisol, the stress hormone, while at the same time increasing the release of oxytocin, also known as the "love" or "trust" hormone.

Specifically, oxytocin has been found to increase self-esteem, optimism, and generosity; build trust; and foster bonding. Studies show that a rise in oxytocin can relieve pain (ah, that's where my headache went!) and has anti-inflammatory properties too.

When we receive or give touch, the same areas of the brain light up as those that are activated when we smell something we like or taste sweet things. Hugs reward the brain in the same way that a piece of chocolate might.

Finding Touch

If you're not in a relationship, don't have family close by, or your friends aren't the hugging type, getting the physical touch you need can be difficult. Maybe you do have some close contact, the odd dry handshake and quick hug, but it's not enough, and you feel vulnerable and awkward asking for the type of gentle touch you crave. (Note: That's important—*ask*, don't take.)

Well, first know that you aren't alone in experiencing this skin loneliness. I received dozens of messages just from people in my own social network when I asked if anyone felt deprived of touch. Do a quick Google search and you'll see multiple posts in forums asking for advice on how to seek this platonic touch without entering into a relationship. There are dozens of cuddle parties arranged every year in London, where I live, as more and more people meet up to mutually exchange physical affection in a way that sadly just isn't a usual part of daily life. It's why some individuals work as "professional cuddlers," offering therapeutic touch in exchange for $80 an hour.

If this isn't for you, there are other ways to get the healing touch you need—visiting a bodyworker or a masseuse. You could join a partner-based dance class or get a pet. In the meantime, just lovingly rubbing in moisturizer after a bath in a way that feels luxurious to the skin can be a tactile treat. Simple activities like a bath can be transformed just through the beauty of intention—and through deliberately feeling your skin, the soap suds, the heat of the water, and how your body relaxes under your own touch. Place a hand on your belly and one on your heart, sink into the hot water, and relax.

See if you can summon up the courage to offer a hug when the moment next feels right. You might get a no, but on the upside, it might make someone's day. I was outside a train station once when a homeless man came up to me asking for change. I had no cash on me, but he looked pretty dejected, so I asked if he wanted a hug. He nodded, and

I gave him a hug. When I pulled away, he was crying. I think my heart broke a little bit that day.

Food

I have one overarching philosophy that applies to both food and sex: Whatever you choose to put or not put in your mouth has no impact whatsoever on your value as a human being. Let me say it even clearer: The scales are not a scorecard. Your weight is not your worth.

That being said, most of us could choose to eat in a way that nourishes both mind and body more. We know the benefits of healthy eating. So why is it so hard to do? Well, it's complicated.

Food is fuel, yes, but it's also a sensory pleasure, a cultural signifier, a social activity, and a way to bond. It can be a creative outlet, a coping mechanism, a source of guilt, a mission, or a moral code.

On top of that exhausting melee, from the moment we're born, we're bombarded with contradictory conscious and subconscious messages on how to feel about food.

By the time you reach your eighteenth birthday, you will have had 33,000 learning experiences with food (based on three meals and a couple of snacks a day).

That's one hell of a relationship history to unravel.

Learning how to behave around food differently, if that is what you want or need to do to help your body, is not something that happens overnight. But it is doable. I know because I've been there. I have eating disorders in my family and have had disordered eating myself; I've put on 65 lb. and lost it—and gained it and lost it. My eating feels good sometimes, and other times, I slip back into old patterns.

Often, when we're really focused or excited, we forget to eat at all. Sometimes, I'm so buzzed or absorbed by what I'm doing that I stop checking in with the body that allows me to do those things. I don't want to lose the flow of how I'm feeling, so I hold on tight to whatever emotional high I'm riding and then crash later. It's not a caring thing to do for my body.

We can be emotional eaters too. I use pizza as a solution when hunger isn't the problem. So I'll eat when I'm sad or lonely: hot mushrooms and cheese as a substitute for a loving hug and a shoulder to cry on.

Sometimes we eat because we're tired or stressed. Chocolate chip cookies aren't known for their ability to make reading about Brexit less complicated, or for solving an argument with your sister, but, hey, I use them like that.

Biologically, it sort of makes sense that many of us might eat like this. When we eat food, dopamine—a feel-good neurotransmitter, or chemical in the brain—gets released. This activates the reward and pleasure centers in the brain. Certain foods give us a particularly sharp spike in dopamine, including foods high in fat and sugar.

Then, over time, we come to associate feeling good with certain foods. We reach for a chocolate bar every time something stressful happens, and we start to feel anxious. Biology prompts behavior that becomes a habit. At that point, we coast away on circular autopilot, eating how we've always eaten because we've always eaten that way.

This is a very simplified version of the relationship between food, body, and mind in an area that is crowded with rapidly expanding research. The best I can do is explain how I changed my own eating to serve me better.

Befriend Your Food

This is about adjusting your relationship to food; just as you would do in a relationship with a person, it makes sense to get to know your food too. There's a *lot* of information out there, and not all of it is helpful.

At the end of the day, for me, it's just been about getting savvy with basic nutritional information and finding out what I'm eating, and why certain foods might make me feel good or bad, happy or grumpy. Taking an interest and making informed choices.

It means knowing that certain fruits contain more sugar than others—mango is a fruit with lots of sugar in it, and the same is true for grapes. Strawberries and blueberries less so. In general, the more tropical a fruit is, or the hotter the climate it grows in, the more sugar it is likely to contain.

It means accepting that added sugar is added sugar and therefore means calories, no matter what form that sugar takes. Fruit juice is full of sugar, even if it's just juiced fruit.

Sweet, natural foods like honey can have some additional health benefits, such as antibacterial properties. At the end of the day, it is still sugar, though—and there's plenty of research that shows too much sugar is not good for our bodies.

Sugar is one type of carbohydrate. Starch is another. Carbohydrates provide the body with energy.

Some vegetables have more carbs than others. Green, leafy vegetables have fewer carbs; root vegetables—the ones that grow underground—have more carbs.

There's a difference, however, between carbs in vegetables and "refined carbs" in bread and sweets. Refined-carb foods cause a spike in energy levels, which initially feels great, until you crash and want more—starting a craving cycle.

Refined carbs have had the fiber stripped out; they've been processed, which is not great, as fiber is good for the gut; fiber helps clean out the gut. Things like oats have lots of fiber in them—soluble fiber that turns into a gel in the gut, can prevent fat from being absorbed, and slows down digestion, which can stop energy spikes. There's also insoluble fiber, which can't be digested at all but speeds up the movement and processing of waste. Foods high in insoluble fiber include kidney beans, popcorn, and wheat bran. Fiber is also thought to make you feel full; it can be found in nuts too—another nutritious food. They are high in calories, though.

Knowing which foods are high in calories can help guide your eating, if you're watching your energy intake.

Five Valuable Tips for Eating Well

1. Plan: If there are times you're tempted by fast food or takeout, get stuff that is easy to eat and that you like, so you have a nice option for yourself too.
2. Don't cut off your legs because you fell over once. So you had some food that wasn't so healthy. That's okay! You don't have to give up and eat all the pizza in the world now.
3. Have some high-quality distractions—if you eat when you're bored, make sure you have other things to do that are just as tempting.
4. Drink more water. Buy a water bottle, and keep it with you at all times.
5. Carry good snacks around with you (such as a banana or a small bag of nuts or seeds).

Knowing which foods contain certain vitamins and minerals and what those vitamins and minerals do for the body can be useful too. For example, spinach and apricots (even some dark chocolate) contain iron—which contributes to the healthy oxygen in red blood cells.

Food can affect mood. Spinach is also thought to be good for anxiety, as it contains a lot of magnesium. Some refer to the gut as the "second brain"—there are more than a billion neurons lining our enteric nervous system, which stretches from our esophagus to our anus and is 30 feet long. That's more neurons, or nerve cells, than are in our spinal cord; it's thought that we have that many so that the brain doesn't have to get too involved with the complicated process of digestion—the gut has a basic knowledge of what to do itself.

We know that our moods affect our stomach (think about how when we're excited we feel butterflies, when we're nervous we might feel sick, or when we're very anxious we may need to go to the toilet), but we're only just beginning to scratch the surface of how our gut bacteria affect our mood. For example, one small study showed that women who ate a bacteria-containing yogurt for a month had changes in parts of the brain that process emotion, suggesting a decrease in anxiety.[8]

Oranges are also thought to be a great mood booster because of the high amounts of vitamin B12 as well as vitamin C (though red peppers have more vitamin C than oranges). Part of getting friendly with your food might mean knowing that fruits and vegetables that are orange and yellow have beta-carotene in them (think carrots) and the body can turn it into vitamin A—which, among other things, is good for eye health.

I now know that certain oils are awesome for my brain, which loves fatty acids such as omega-3s and omega-6s, and that this oil comes in fish and nuts.

Supermarket Shopping

Befriending my food meant I started getting curious about what was in my food and where it came from. I began being that person reading the backs of the packages in the supermarket. Then I started not being very impressed with the copious list of unintelligible ingredients in prepared foods. I started wanting to cook more rather than eat things that were mass produced. I realized fat-free doesn't mean fewer calories and that fewer calories doesn't mean fewer carbs.

I struggle to eat a lot of meat now after a particularly gruesome discovery I made as a journalist about exactly how slaughterhouses operated. Reading more about how factory farming works, it sat so sickly in my stomach, well, I don't really want chlorine-washed chicken anytime soon. I only eat meat from farms that are approved by animal welfare organizations.

Sure, sometimes I get lazy and go pick up something quick and tasteless from the supermarket that can be heated up in five minutes. But now that I know what's in that food, it makes it all the harder to skip out on choosing what's best for my body. Choosing the packaged meal feels like a less caring thing to do for myself because I'm aware of what's nourishing. Finding out the benefits of what I ate encouraged me to make loving decisions about what I put in my mouth.

Know How It Feels

Once you've gotten to know a little bit about how food works in theory, it's good to tune into the experience of eating that food and discovering your preferences.

Start with how it feels in your mouth. The rubbery, slimy, fibrous sensation that accompanies chewing on a banana—

the slightly sticky after-texture that it leaves in your mouth. The cleansing, acidic taste of lemon, which can sting your palette into seminumbness. A dense yet crumbly cheese. The injection of sweet juice that squirts across your palate as you burst a grape between your teeth.

I started to chew and digest mindfully, rather than chomping manically. Could I relish every mouthful? What would happen if I slowed down while I consumed?

I made sure I ate sitting down, without reading or watching TV, and just have eating be what it was. I started to notice what the sensation of being satisfied felt like in my body.

I checked in with myself to see which foods not only tasted delicious while I was eating them but also felt good in my body afterward. How mashed potatoes gave me this warm heavy feeling, how eggs got me energized but stable. How tomatoes made me feel … horny.

I also noticed it actually feels better if I don't eat certain foods—even if my creature pretends it's craving them. Sugar is my nemesis, my gateway drug to neglectful eating. One brownie and I just can't stop. I'll have dessert in restaurants, but otherwise I won't keep sugar in the house. For me, it's addictive. Every time I have it, it takes another week for the cravings to wear off again, to stop being irritable and restless because I'm not having cake for breakfast.

One thing I noticed as I gathered facts about food and tuned in to the feelings was that I seemed to have an awful lot of ideas about food that were more than just science and sensation. My pantry was fully stocked with stories too.

Unraveling Your Food Fairy Tales

See if you can catch yourself telling yourself stories about food. Are potatoes the enemy? Is cake a rebellious treat and fruit a boring obligation?

When I'm loading my plate with meaning as well as complex carbohydrates, it affects not only my choices but also how I enjoy my food and sometimes even how I feel about myself.

So I began to deconstruct the narrative, and either challenge it or change it for one that served me better.

I wanted food to feel less like a guilty pleasure and more like what it was: nutrition. If you want to do this, ask yourself if you can make foods that nourish you feel like a treat. Give your food a good story, an attractive one. I repackaged blueberries as a superfood in my head, looked up all their nutritional benefits, remembered they were expensive—therefore valuable—and said "yes" to all of these things with every mouthful. Unsurprisingly, they tasted a lot better.

Tell Yourself Any Story That Works for You

What I will say is: Make sure your story is positive. There are three reasons for that:

1. There are already too many unhappy stories in this world. Trust me, I'm a journalist. Let's not add to them with ones we've created deliberately to punish ourselves. No one needs more negative stories in their brains.

2. Our nervous system has two responses to help us live safe and happy lives. One is the sympathetic nervous system—the "fight or flight" response. The other is the para-sympathetic nervous system—this allows us to relax and feel calm. If the sympathetic nervous system is activated, the body cannot digest food—after all, if you're being chased by a bear, it's not really of immediate importance to metabolize; it's much better to shift the energy to arms and legs, so you can make your life-or-death decisions. The thing is, we can go into this primitive survival mode if we are stressed or even if we beat ourselves up through anxiety—and this then makes it much harder for us to digest the nutrients from our food. It also encourages our body to hoard fat. Much better then, if we are eating, to consider how delicious and wonderful the food is, than make ourselves feel guilty.

3. Food is enjoyable. Eating can be an immense pleasure. I cannot see any purpose in any activity that denies, diminishes, or demonizes our appetites. If you're eating for the joy of eating, in a way that respects your body, it's unlikely that you will overindulge. Distortions occur when, like I did, you use food as a focus to distract you from uncomfortable emotional states, or you eat so fast you don't feel full.

Food matters. It affects how we feel and how we are fueled physically. The nutrients we absorb can affect our mood, and our mood can affect our digestion. Learning the basics about food, the scientific nuts and bolts of nutrition, and observing how we feel physically and emotionally when we eat a certain way, can help inform our diet. Every body is different, and eating what feels good for you might be different from what feels good for me. Essentially, food is this wonderful tool that can support your emotional and physical health and is also pleasurable. Whoop!

Feed yourself. Nourish yourself. Enjoy yourself, with food.

Nature

Getting outside and into nature is the most underrated activity that benefits your body and your mind—and your soul. And it's free, most of the time.

To be fair, its image has had a bit of a revamp recently, what with coverage of wellness treatments like "forest bathing" (standing with trees to make you feel better) and eco-therapy (getting outside and doing something active), but we've still got a long way to go before we give the wealth and beauty of nature the same social importance as the culture and buzz of the city.

There's a tendency to associate urban centers with investment, progress and talent, and the countryside with isolation, retreat and stagnation. It's somewhat of a self-fulfilling prophecy in terms of the economics of it all.

Yet, money aside, this view fails to take into account the life-affirming, sense-awakening, mind-freshening nature of greenery.

If you give a f★★k about your mental health, about your body, about how you stay alive, you have to care about nature. And not just in the abstract, buying sustainable produce and shopping for organic food, but by actually getting out there. Get outside and get some green (not that one). Connect with your wild side. It's where you came from, and it's where you're going back to.

Perhaps that's why we're a little shy. It reminds us that we're smaller than we sometimes like to think. That even the big man in his big job in his big office, feeling smug at his big maple-wood desk, is the same as any of us in the maple-wood forest.

That isn't something to fear. I think of being in these humbling landscapes as an outlook bomb: You know the ones—they go off in your brain sometimes, something clicks about what is really true and important, and it totally explodes your perspective, shifting your outlook. There's a lot we can learn from nature about the way to live.

While walking in the countryside and observing the way trees and bushes grow to fill the space available, I realize nature doesn't question who it is, or what it is, whether it should or shouldn't be there, it just *is* and it expands to be the most it can possibly be in the space it's given. Seeing vines snake up a rock face, or branches that bend in the wind, I think about how we, too, could learn from their generosity in the face of adversity; they don't fight it, but flex with it. How we could seek to adapt to changes in our external circumstances, in the landscape of our own lives, with similar grace. Nature only seeks to keep growing, to keep being what it is to the best of its ability, developing around obstacles in its path, and making those impediments beautiful simply by its presence. It overcomes them simply by growing.

Nothing is "wrong" in nature—it embraces everything. There is a part for everything in the ecosystem. Nothing ever dies; it simply changes form and returns back to the forest floor. With such abundance, perhaps that's why it doesn't wait to be asked to give to you, but nourishes your being as soon as you enter its soft, ferny fronds, without ever expecting anything in return. Replenishing is the way to go, and it doesn't question whether that's fair or right, but just follows its instinct. I sometimes think that love is our essential nature too; we just get a bit distracted by all the fear and busyness and forget to be ourselves. Luckily, the option is always there to remember— just try to be moved by inspiration rather than by desperation, although desperation was how I found the joy in nature again.

Take Off Your Shoes and Socks

I'm not sure when I first realized I was so thirsty for nature— I think it was while I was doing the last six months of my news editing job and there was this horrible push-pull between wanting to do it and not just do it, but do it really well—all the while knowing that it wasn't right for me. I spent those six months throwing myself at something that I was simultaneously repelled by. The headlines weren't making it any easier—excruciating misery and arguing politicians, as usual. I felt drained.

I live and work in Central London, and while it's not the smog-filled beast of industrial Victoriana, it can be a little bald on the nature front if you don't go looking for it. I found myself wandering to the park every lunchtime, as if magnetically pulled by the trees and water away from the painful chaos of the news. Walking on the path with other people wasn't enough. I had to run into the wooded areas and actually feel myself surrounded. To stroke the leaves, touch the rough bark, to take my shoes and socks off, and feel the grass beneath my feet. I realized I hadn't done this in months. My toes didn't know what the earth felt like.

We don't think of being outdoors in nature as something vital, and yet this word comes from the Latin *vitalis*, meaning "of, or belonging to, life"—and what is more alive than nature? Those lunchtimes in the park where I covered my calves with crunchy leaves and spoke to squirrels were the only thing that saved me from the ugliness in the headlines poisoning my heart. The simplicity and connection in the wild order of nature, the power independent of human meddling, I found intensely restorative.

We know this intuitively, but studies show it too. People living close to trees and green spaces are less likely to be obese, inactive, or taking antidepressants.[9] Nature-based activities can also help people who are suffering from mental health problems and can help reduce levels of anxiety, stress, and depression.[10] There's an increasing body of research in this area, as more and more of us come to realize that the soothing effects of being surrounded by beautiful landscapes is not a "nice extra" but a necessity for our own well-being, and scientists seek to prove it.

> The oldest living organism in the world is a tree—or trees. It's called Pando, or Trembling Giant, and is a colony of aspen trees spread over 106 acres. It's in Utah and its root system shows it's actually one individual organism that's 80,000 years old.

What I love about nature is that when you're outside, you're never alone. Not really. Everything around you is instinctive, living wilderness, and yet has a place and a purpose. It's bigger than you and yet you are part of it. It's hard not to be comforted by that when it feels like it's you against a world where everything is wrong and everyone is hurting. It draws from me a long exhale. I think the plants make us feel like this on purpose so they can get their CO_2. Their best interests are our best interests too.

Try making it your mission to get to know all the green spaces in your area, so that you have a good idea of where to go if you start to feel burnt out. Develop favorites. Commit to spending twenty minutes in one, at least once a week. While there, take a look at the trees and grass and what's around you and see what lessons you can learn from the way nature adapts and grows in the environment. Touch the grass beneath you, or the bark of a tree for five seconds with the palm of your hand (even if you feel a little silly).

Imagination

Consider the imagination as an unseen muscle for magic—the genitals of the brain, if you will. Like our reproductive organs, the imagination is the birthplace of creativity, with the same dark power of sexual energy. Too many of us abuse our incredible capacity for imagination, spending most of our lives throwing its might on the useless and the banal or constructing our own personal mental hell. We have imaginary arguments with our boss or our colleagues—or daydream about what's for dinner. While there's nothing wrong with expending your imagination on such pursuits, only exercising them like this is the equivalent of using a silk couture gown to clean your toilet.

Similarly, using your imagination solely for escapism is a little like junk food for your soul. Imagination lives at the border between reality and dreams—it's a flying machine that carries visions as its cargo, transporting fantasies from one realm into another. It's not meant to issue one-way tickets.

Imagination holds no prejudice or preference. It will carry light or dark across this veil—it will import genius or madness, with the power to infect or transform our worlds. Use it well.

It's clear there's something a little bit special about our imagination—the ability to conjure and connect concepts, pictures, symbols, and movies that may not yet exist. This power just doesn't follow common-sense rules. Consider this:

★ Children are better at it than adults.
★ It speeds up when we slow down—and is most productive when we are least productive, feeding off boredom, quietness, and solitude.
★ It is the most effective way we create change and is also the main thing responsible for holding us back.
★ It constructs and destructs.

Society has mixed feelings about imagination and has attempted to repress, constrain, and degrade its power. Daydreaming is considered unproductive, funding is funneled away from the arts, and we've almost lost the concept of a visionary as anything other than a rich technology CEO. One thing we can determine is that anything this maligned must be very powerful.

In fact, more and more academics are proposing that it is our capacity for imagination that specifically makes us human. Anthropologist Agustín Fuentes argues that the ability to imagine and to take that imagination and make it into reality is one of the things that is *really* distinctive about humans.[11] Clive Gamble, author of *Settling the Earth: The Archaeology of Deep Human History*, argues that our ability to imagine other worlds was what led humans toward global expansion and exploration.[12] "Rather than being coldly rational, our pioneering ancestors were warmly relational—making connections between people, places, and things. It was out of that imaginative mix that looking further than the horizon became attractive."

Sir Ken Robinson goes even further, saying, "Imagination, I believe, is what fundamentally sets us apart from the rest of life on Earth—very little does, truthfully."[13]

With that in mind, it's important that we respect and use this incredible capacity in a way that honors our humanity, that serves both us and the world.

That means taking a step back to reevaluate if the main use of your imagination is to indulge in endless worrying, conjuring your own personal disaster scenario at every junction of uncertainty in your life. Our bodies can't tell the difference between a genuine threat and a horror movie. Ever had that experience of dreaming that you fought with someone, only to wake up and still be mad at them over the breakfast table? Or does imagining some scenarios bring tears to your eyes, and leave your body feeling tight and your breath constricted, even though the reality is that, right now, things are pretty damn good?

When I was a little girl, I discovered this peculiar way that your emotions and body can react to what you think about, not just what's actually going on. I was in a classroom and, seeing me sobbing, the teacher came over to ask if I was okay. I brightened up and said proudly,

"Yes, I just worked out I can make myself cry!" "Oh," she replied. "How did you do that?" "I imagined my whole family was murdered," I told her. I think they spoke to my mom that day.

Toxic Dreams and Fighting Ghosts

As someone who carried this vivid imagination into adulthood, I realize it's not as easy as just "stopping worrying." However, three realizations helped take the edge off this toxic habit.

The first was that, far from preparing me for difficult situations in the future, it was actually lowering my self-esteem. I had come to believe that using my imagination to anticipate possible shortcomings or downfalls was helping me plan for the future and protect me from negative outcomes. There may have been times when it picked up a few possible threats. Most of the time, though, it just kept me locked in my own personal hellscape, and the damaging message that lay beneath these catastrophic imaginings was that I was not enough. Not strong enough, not powerful enough, not clever enough to respond to whatever came up in life in real time, without going through this imaginary overpreparation first. There came a point where my mental insurance approach was taking too much of a toll on me. Instead, I now use uncertainty as a chance to practice self-belief—to trust in myself that, whatever happens, I have enough, I know enough, I am enough, to take the right course of action in any given situation.

The second realization was that a not-so-useful arrogance was propelling this activity. I had inflated my power in worrying—playing a kind of impotent "I told you so" game with myself, where I would select only the negative and then tell myself, "Oh, look, bad things happened, therefore I was right to worry." I would also tell myself, "Oh, everything turned out great, therefore I was right to worry; it probably saved the situation."

This rationale is illustrated wonderfully in a story involving a train, two men, and toilet paper. A backpacker gets on a train in India, where, as soon as they leave the station, he witnesses an old man reach down into his shopping bag and take out a toilet paper roll. The old man then stands up, opens the window, and begins to tear off sheet after sheet, throwing it through the window as the train flies through the countryside. The tourist watches him do this for fifteen minutes without interruption. But as he nears his stop, he summons up the courage to ask the man why he has been engaged in this bizarre activity. "I'm stopping elephants from crossing the tracks," says the old man. "How can that stop the elephants?" the traveler replies. "Well, have you seen an elephant yet?" is the response.

That's the thing about worry rituals—we think they help, but the reality is they're doing nothing but have us buy into an illusion of control. The price for that illusion is feeling tight and suspicious much of the time. It's a pretty bad deal, right?

Messy environments can produce more creative thought than neat and orderly ones. One experiment showed that people in disorderly environments tended to be more creative and think outside the box more. However, if you want to try *clean eating* or be more conscientious, the opposite is true—more orderly environments are beneficial.[14]

This worry ritual is observed especially when it comes to one particular preoccupation I call "fighting ghosts." These are imaginary arguments, a peculiar fusion of words, characters, and pictures that allow us to fight with our projections of people. I can't count the number of ghosts I've fought over the years—I regularly used to spend the bus ride to work having imaginary arguments with my boss, colleagues, or old boyfriends, anticipating things they might say or do and my rejoinder to those things. It is, for the most part, not only a monumental waste of time and energy, but also brings out the worst in ourselves and others. When we expect others to attack us, it leaks into our attitude, behavior and tone. We end up walking around covered in spikes, defensive and offensive, and resentful at things that haven't even happened. So if you spend any of your time fighting ghosts, stop it now. Stop cultivating a superpower that activates people's lowest common denominator. When it comes to relationships, very rarely can you solve a problem that hasn't happened yet.

The truth is, the majority of your worry is not only useless but fosters a self-perception that is both arrogant and insecure.

Working with Your Imagination

So, what to do instead? Well, the mind doesn't like emptiness, so it's very hard to rid it of an imagined grim scenario without replacing it with something else. So how about instead of imagining what you *don't want*, imagine what you *do want*?

This was my third realization: I could ask myself what would be the ideal scenario instead. I would begin just by posing these questions: If I could make anything happen, what would it be? What do I really want? Once I had a starting point, I'd begin fleshing out the details. I use the word "flesh" on purpose—get visceral with it. Imagine what you would be seeing, hearing, feeling. See if you can get really specific. And then make it vivid, turning the colors up, the volume up. Make it as real as possible. Almost live it.

Sometimes it's hard to pinpoint what I want—and that's a humbling experience: to realize that I'm so focused on the scenario I *don't want* to play out that I forget to get in touch with what I hope will happen. It's like trying to use a map that only has where you *don't want to go* marked on it—it's impossible to navigate—and your focus is constantly pulled to the very thing you actually want to avoid.

Other times, I build these imaginary empires in my mind, but it's hard for the feelings to come. I begin to think to myself: "I wonder if I actually want this—I'm not actually feeling very excited." Then I start to imagine something else, and there's a lot of emotion that comes up. That's when I think, "Wow, there's something for me here." Even if the first is a five-star Caribbean holiday and the second is going home for a week to see the dogs.

Now, I'm not saying that you should never pay attention to these worst-case scenarios served up by your imagination, particularly if you're a firefighter, a doctor, or a schoolteacher or if your job depends on risk assessment. What I am saying is that we use these imaginings either to create a safety net for ourselves or to turn that fear around to show us what we truly love and want to aim for. Try this: When you go to bed tonight, imagine all the things you want to happen in your life—the ideal scenarios. Paint them as vividly as possible, with lots of detail.

There's one last thing that's absolutely key when it comes to how we use our imagination, and that's the ability it gives us to put ourselves in a different position and see things from a different perspective. It allows us to empathize with others, to try to understand how other people might be feeling by imagining ourselves in that situation. This ability is vital for forming connections with other people—which is where caring about yourself becomes really challenging: in relationships.

Relationships

GIVE A F**K ABOUT RELATIONSHIPS

It's hard to give a f★★k about anything effectively if you don't also care about relating to people. There are 7 billion people in the world. You are going to bump into some of them. Might as well learn how to bump into them so that everyone gets the most out of the experience.

"Bump" is a good word for it. Relationships are not always easy to navigate—we clash, fight, and cry. That's why there's a lot in this section that deals with, shall we say, euphemistically, the "tricky" parts of relating. (For "tricky," read "often screaming into the sky with frustration.") To care about relationships in a way that helps us expand as people and get the loving connections we crave, we need to know first how to set boundaries, how to say "no," how to avoid blame, and how to be truthful with one another; caring about your connections in such a way that you don't abandon your own needs or demonize others' desires is a practice, and it's not about perfection. It's a bit like yoga—you do it, even though at first it might be uncomfortable and you feel like a fool and it sure as hell stretches you. The rewards are worth it, though.

We need people, and we need relationships. Lord knows, I've tried to do life without intimacy, without close friends, without partnerships or passion. I've even tried to keep love at a distance, simply because I didn't know how to care without every quarrel, misunderstanding, and separation overwhelming—and devastating—my whole life and my heart along with it.

But life without relationships is like profiteroles without delicious chocolate sauce: dry, bland, and chewy. Humans are social creatures—we've evolved to connect and be with each other; it gives us something we yearn for as people, a special nutrient for survival that we can't access alone. Relationships are the lubricant that helps make life more than a series of interesting events. They call us out to engage with the wider world and make both our internal and external experiences brighter, more vivid, more alive—even if sometimes that intensity feels excruciating.

You can't do relationships without the risk of pain— all you can do is learn how to keep yourself safe and care about learning from those experiences. Not in a kind of "never again with them" way (although that might be the case sometimes), but rather to teach you about yourself and how to connect with love.

Personal relationships are great for growth. They allow us to see our raw, sore spots, the places we still won't accept ourselves, where we project our judgments onto others and where we withdraw our love or friendship. If we can stay alert, we will also be shown situations that trigger us, where we still knee-jerk and lash out with fear, rather than being vulnerable, honest and sinking into love. It's only by seeing this that we can change things. Intimacy—being in close contact with people—can polish us, sloughing off our rough edges and transforming us from rough-hewn granite into shiny, smooth, beautiful pebbles.

For me, pride was one of the first things to be sanded off, along with a need to be always right. Relationships are ripe with opportunities for mistake-making, which is wonderful for taking the ego out of the driver's seat and useful because f★★king things up gives you an opportunity to get really good at making amends again. It also gives you a chance to practice forgiveness and notice the places where your heart is still a bit hard and closed off to love.

Boundaries

Ever met one of those people who doesn't respect personal space? They always seem to corner you at parties. You strike up a conversation, but they're leaning so far in that you edge away to feel comfortable, only to have them bend toward you again. Before you know it, you're doing this shuffling dance around the entire room, feeling vaguely invaded, until you mercifully bump into the drinks table and conjure up a swift excuse to escape.

This is a small-scale example of what happens when boundaries are not respected, or communicated: discomfort, collision, and, ultimately, disconnection.

Boundaries are fundamental to how we relate. They mark our limits: where we end and the other person begins and vice versa. They can be physical or spatial—like the earlier example. They can be emotional or mental—the appropriate separation of our feelings, thoughts, and opinions. Boundaries are usually consciously set in romantic relationships. For example, in a monogamous pairing, you might agree to be sexually intimate only with your current partner (the "exclusive" chat) until you both decide otherwise. There are boundaries around property: This is my land; that is yours. We have boundaries around our bodies: People aren't allowed to touch us if we don't want them to. Importantly, the last two are examples of boundaries protected by law. In this section, I'm talking about less clear-cut cases, but make no mistake, our boundaries are vital.

In relationships, clear boundaries help define what the other person can expect from you and what you can expect from the other person. Your own boundaries form the bottom line of what you will and won't accept, based on what you need to feel free, safe, and fulfilled.

Boundaries are something of a paradox. Far from separating us, the act of dividing what's yours and what's mine actually creates more intimacy, not less. Healthy boundaries strengthen the connection between people, allowing them to communicate more effectively and work together smoothly. Clear boundaries encourage people to take responsibility for themselves, to develop their own sense of self in security. Boundaries delineate the rules of engagement, providing a safe structure to allow people to move closer to each other. Without healthy boundaries, people feel invaded and resentful; they disengage and burn out.

This is a highly charged and delicate topic—failing to respect boundaries leaves us feeling violated, yet often we aren't taught about them and struggle to identify our own boundaries until they are crossed. We don't always know how to communicate boundaries effectively—and even when they are communicated, we fail to honor them with our actions. Plus, our boundaries are different with different people; there's no fixed set of rules so that we can learn to avoid making mistakes. To top it all off, boundaries *shift*—both in individual relationships and within ourselves. It's not easy to keep up!

First, don't beat yourself up if you discover you've either disrespected your own boundaries or those of others. In the tectonic world of boundaries, we are all violators and have been violated. Setting and respecting personal boundaries is my personal kryptonite—and here are some examples where mine get fuzzy:

★ "Yes, it is totally fine to turn up late for our coffee date every time, and, no, I won't say anything."
★ "Sure, you can email me after hours in a demanding tone, and I will always respond."

★ "Yes, I'll come over and babysit for free even though I'm late on this work deadline and your child is a horror."

★ "Okay, Mom. You can show up at my house without asking and then decide to clean it." ("Oh, you didn't want me to tidy up all your personal papers without asking? I'm so sorry.")

★ "Oh, should I have asked before I brought my partner to dinner too?"

★ "I thought it was fine that I borrowed your top; it didn't seem like you really wore it that much."

Maybe these scenarios feel familiar to you. If you want to build satisfying and nourishing relationships, you *need* to care about boundaries. Set your boundaries too loose and you'll end up doing way too much, worn out and tired with no energy for things you want to achieve. (People who can't say "no," I'm looking at you.) If we don't know how to set boundaries, sometimes we end up building walls around us, which let no one in and, hello, isolation and loneliness (people who struggle to say "yes").

How to Spot if You Struggle with Boundaries
★ Are you often late?
★ Do you often find yourself overly irritated by others' lateness?
★ Do you often feel tired and like you have no time for yourself?
★ Do you flake on people at the last minute?
★ Do you ever "ghost" dates?

★ Do you frequently shut people out or ignore them?

★ Do you ever feel responsible for someone else's happiness?

★ Do you think if someone else is unhappy it is "your job" to make them feel better?

★ Do you ever attribute your unhappiness to someone else?

★ Have you ever been accused of oversharing or interfering?

★ Do you find it impossible to maintain or share your good mood if someone around you is in a bad mood?

★ Do you feel other people's feelings are more important than your own?

★ Do you rarely lose your temper but, when you do, you explode?

★ Do you feel constantly bogged down by feelings of guilt?

★ Do you feel like the only safe place for you to relax is when you are on your own?

If you said "yes" to two or more of these, it might be that you have some confusion around boundaries. What should help your relationships be less climactic and more connected is establishing what is your responsibility, what is not, and learning how to say "no." I'll cover all this in the following sections.

Knowing What's Yours

For a long time, I had zero emotional boundaries. I might have been walking around masquerading as a separate human being—with my own feelings, dreams, problems, and needs—but actually I was just a supersensitive radio tower, humming with everyone else's music. If they were happy, I was happy. If they were sad, I was disturbed. I only understood the phrase "not my problem" in theory— if something was within my radius, it would nag for my attention until I became involved. I internalized the needs of others—it felt like my job to make everyone get along. Only then did I feel settled.

When you struggle with boundaries, it becomes difficult to work out what's yours and what belongs to other people.

> Though the concept of personal boundaries is nothing new (think of the Bible on personal responsibility—"you reap what you sow"), it's only really been popular as part of counseling or self-help work since the 1980s.

Do you have some days where you wake up and it's as if you've forgotten to put your skin on? When every single emotion you come into contact with—from reading an angry post on Facebook to an upset friend on the phone—jangles your entire system, until, by the end of the day, you feel overwhelmed and heavy and you're not really sure why? It's like you're a tuning fork for dozens of dissonant emotional vibrations that you can't seem to shut out, and so you just reverberate into the ground and then shut down, exhausted.

Your Feelings Are Your Feelings—Their Feelings Are Their Feelings

Each of us is ultimately responsible for how we feel. What we tell ourselves, how we interpret situations and how we respond to whatever is going on is what causes us to feel the way we do.

If we're stressed by a deadline—that's our stress. No one planted the feelings in our body. If we're happy—that's ours too; we showed up and allowed ourselves to feel free. If we're upset, that's our emotional processes at work—it's not someone else's job to reverse the event to make our feelings change. If we feel guilty about the way someone else feels—that's our guilt. No one "made" you feel anything, and neither are you solely responsible for anyone else's emotional turbulence.

Our feelings are directed by our own deeply personal inner processes. People can feel differently about the same events, depending on their past history, their beliefs, their mood that day.

But what about upsetting people? Well, it happens. You can't control that, but you can adjust what you make it mean about you as a person, or how you respond to having accidentally hurt someone's feelings. Just say what's true for you at any given moment and let people react how they wish. They are allowed to feel how they want to too. It's their life and their experience. Respect that.

Getting in Touch with Yourself

It's human to sympathize, but it isn't healthy to take on everybody else's feelings as your own. For a start, it's exhausting: We have enough trouble processing our own emotions without having to work through a ghostly imprint of everyone else's too. Even if you're not conscious of doing it, you may begin to feel crazy because you feel awful but can't identify why—plus there's not very much you can do about adjusting those negative emotions, because they weren't even yours to begin with.

Extreme emotional contagion is actually the death of compassion. It may lead to resentment, as you forget that someone in pain isn't demanding you to experience their pain too. You might isolate yourself, because being around groups of people is too much with all their different feelings, problems, and needs. Or maybe you develop a need to control people and situations excessively to maintain a sense of your own equilibrium.

This is the dark side to not having appropriate emotional boundaries. If you need other people to feel okay in order to feel okay yourself, then you are going to end up having to manipulate and suppress other people's feelings. It's not about sorting out the world so that you can feel good. It's about developing your own internal processes for feeling good and then bringing that joy to those parts of the world that want it.

It's easy to say, but if you've spent a large portion of your life being very good at watching and gauging other people's emotional states, you may have no idea how to feel your own emotions. You might be great at pleasing people or knowing their anger triggers, but there's a gaping void in the place of your personal feelings about an issue. You can change this; it just takes practice.

Start Slow

Set an alarm on your phone three times a day, so that you can check in and ask yourself, "How do I feel right now?" See if you can come up with two emotions and where you feel them in your body. If you can't name the feeling, just see if you can describe physical sensations. This process is important, even though it is hard at first, because if you are in touch with how your own feelings *feel* inside your body, it's easier to recognize when you're starting to take on an emotion that's not yours.

Your Problems Are Your Problems—Their Problems Are Their Problems

This might sound harsh, but no one is obliged to solve your problems. No one has to listen to you, and no one *has* to give you sympathy.

"Ah," you might think, "but what about my partner? Surely I should expect them to cheer me up!"

Nope. It is not their duty to make you happy. It is no one's job to rescue you from your own life. You can tell them how you would like to be listened to and you can ask for advice or support, but it is their choice whether they decide to offer any. They might have had a bad day too. They might need to attend to their own problems. You are both adults, even if that makes two grumpy adults sitting in silence, taking ten minutes to thaw out before they can be available for each other.

This might all seem very clinical, and it's important to note that there's nothing wrong with giving. You may enjoy giving. But look at your intention—why you're doing it. Giving out of guilt or obligation, because of a need for validation or with expectation of "payback," are all manipulative recipes for resentment and low self-worth. Similarly, asking from a place of entitlement doesn't allow someone to freely give to you or honor their ability to say "no." Which leads us to the next point.

Your Needs Are Your Needs—Their Needs Are Their Needs

Taking responsibility for your needs means investigating what they are in good time, so that you can get them met from an appropriate source—the one most able to meet them—and before the requirement becomes pressing. It can be hard to ask for help, but it is the kindest thing you can do for yourself and others. Waiting until you are desperate to ask for help sets you up for rejection or suffering if someone exercises their right to say "no." It is not a kind way to treat yourself or others. It's wise to attend to your needs as they arise—a little and often approach—rather than depriving yourself until your emotional world is exploding around you.

If someone says "no," move on and keep asking. Remember, it's not about you personally. See your ability to receive a "no" as empowering—it gives you permission to say "no" when you are not able to say "yes," and it's good practice: You were able to receive a "no" and you didn't self-destruct. It doesn't change how valuable you are.

> The reason they tell you to put on your own oxygen mask first on a plane is because the drop in pressure means that in just a few seconds—perhaps before you have even helped someone else—your brain might stop functioning and cannot even identify basic shapes. You will then need someone else to help you or you will become unconscious.

Ask for help from the place or person that is most able to give you what you want. Stop asking your mom to help you with the thing she has proven herself historically to be bad at, then getting upset when she lets you down. Don't make demands on your partner for something when you know a friend is better at the listening and empathy you need. If one person can't help in the way that you need them to, you can ask someone else for the appropriate help. Your friend, mom, or partner might not be the right choice, but your doctor, lawyer, or accountant might be.

You don't need to mold and shape yourself to every person that comes into your life in order to be liked. You have a right to be yourself, and to have that self feel safe and expressed, and have its needs met. You might not have been able to do that for yourself as a child, but you're an adult now. Reclaim what's yours, let go of what's not, and leave others to do the same.

Boundary Maintenance

Next time you are confronted with a situation where someone is feeling a very strong emotion and you are tempted to take it on yourself, take a deep breath and try this practice:

★ Stabilize yourself—feel your feet heavy on the floor; you can even imagine that roots come out of the soles of your feet and down into the earth.

★ Notice the other person's emotion—say to yourself "he/she is feeling anxious today." Remind yourself: "That's theirs; they are feeling that. I am calm. I do not feel that."

★ Breathe. Notice your own emotional status, rather than getting on their roller coaster.

★ Remind yourself that the other person is allowed to ask for what they want.

★ Imagine covering yourself in clear, bright, gold light from your head to your feet: a force field of protection around you. Remain calm and do not mirror their emotion.

★ After leaving their company, check in with yourself and see how you feel. How much have you taken on? This takes practice for it to become automatic, so don't be discouraged if you find it hard.

Saying "No"

Fundamental to being human in relation to other humans is acknowledging our limits: physical, emotional, and mental. We have our own inner-boundary barometer, which lets us know what is acceptable to us or not. Sometimes our mental chatter interferes, telling us we should agree to something—it's polite, our egos think we can handle it, or we think it will be less hassle to just go along with it. However, our bodies always let us know the true answer. Whether we feel able, right, or safe doing something is a far more primal question than is often acknowledged. Ignoring our limits is arrogant and abusive—both to oneself and to others.

If you can listen hard enough, and practice interpreting the signals given by your body, you'll learn to detect whether doing something is right for you or whether it is breaking a boundary. It happens almost on an energetic level. Over time I am learning to note what happens in my body when I am out of my depth and have gone too far, too fast. I get this shrinking, tight feeling in my upper body and a kind of numbness in my face, plus cold tingles in my belly. Occasionally, the sensation is very intense and I'll feel a jet stream of heat shoot up the front of my body.

This isn't hocus-pocus—you can sense these boundaries in other people too. It's the felt awareness of separation that can make it obvious that someone isn't single or available for romance. It's why there are some friends you just don't get physically close to, or you might not naturally hug. We don't consciously choose not to touch or ask them out; it's just that we can sense it wouldn't be appropriate, or there's some resistance from them to—like an invisible dividing line.

When we misinterpret or fail to listen to these signals, we only notice the existence of a boundary once it's been breached. If we are the violators, we may notice a reaction in the other person, and then we can apologize or take other necessary action to amend the wrong. If one of our boundaries is crossed, a feeling of resentment or abuse usually appears. With the exception of certain serious violations (rape, sexual assault, deliberate physical or emotional threat or abuse) that are prohibited by law, when this happens it's best to take what is happening seriously but avoid assigning blame. It is almost always as much your responsibility to protect, communicate, and assert your boundary—and set consequences if that boundary is broken—as it is the other person's to respect it.

"No Big Deal"

Asserting little boundaries is as vital as putting in place those more definitive borders. We tend to forget these less obvious ones, persuading ourselves that we can or should put up with certain minor infractions, gritting our teeth and getting on with it when the person we sit next to at work leaves a mess all over our desk during the night shift. Or when our roommate doesn't clean the bathtub. When our friend turns up a half-hour late for coffee, then fails to apologize. If we can't lower all the emotion, we might glare or act a little frosty, then moan to someone else later, but we still fail to address and provide an opportunity for resolving the misdemeanor.

These examples are all small things in the grand scheme. However, I find that every time I ignore the quiet voice inside me that says "This is not acceptable to me," some tightness appears in my body. I swallow this little brick of resistance down, but it doesn't go away; it just sinks down and slides in neatly, Tetris-style, slotting in beside the last choked-down "no." And so, bit by bit, unvoiced breach by unvoiced breach, a wall of anger builds inside me. Then I might go out for lunch and the kitchen gets my order wrong. I could assert myself calmly, but at this point, I'm up to my throat in backed-up "nos," at the absolute limit of what I can handle. So the poor waitress gets the full force of anger meant for other people as I spray a week's worth of resentment all over the restaurant.

Telling people, step by step, what is acceptable to you and what is not is a much kinder, more honest way to live, for everyone. Otherwise our lives fill up with things, and we don't actually like or want a single one of them. It saps us of energy—living lives full of other people's junk simply because we didn't say "no."

It can be very tempting to drop everything to help someone every time a request is made—especially if you think that person is in a difficult place or needs you in some way. But you are not the only person in the world able to help and you are not a "bad" person if you don't want to— especially if helping would have a direct negative impact on yourself. Obligation and good deeds don't combine well. One pollutes the other. It's the karmic equivalent of squirting ketchup into a nice, hot bubble bath.

> Linguists argue about whether, in the English language, "yes" and "no" should have a grammatical category of their own. They are considered "sentence words"—where a single word forms a sentence. However, some languages don't have "yes" or "no"—Irish and Finnish, for example. In Finnish, if someone asked you, "Have you read the book?" you would simply reply "I have read the book" or "I have not read the book"—the positive or negative form of the verb is used. This is called an "echo" response.

It's difficult to assert yourself—we fear falling short of someone's expectations. That's okay. Sometimes loving ourselves looks like disappointing other people. Saying no to what we don't want means we have the space to say "yes" to the things we do want. It creates the space for us to do those things with our whole heart. It requires using our voice and making sure our actions reflect our words.

Communicating a Boundary

People are not mind readers. Just because something is okay with you doesn't mean it is acceptable to someone else. It is up to us to communicate our boundaries, so that the other person is made aware, and we can avoid clogging up our consciousness with blame or shame.

Prior to the conversation, consider these things:

1. ***Know what you want***

   These can be difficult interactions, so go into the conversation with a clear idea of what is needed and hold on to that anchor if emotions become heated.

   Example: I want my coworker to stop leaving cups, papers, and old tissues on my desk so that I don't have to clear them up in the morning.

2. ***Know why you are having the conversation***

   Take note of both the positive and negative reasons for setting the boundary. Sure, you don't want dirty mugs on your desk because it's irritating, but why else is it beneficial? To have a more respectful relationship with your colleague? To concentrate more on your work? Know the reasons it is important to you to have a clean desk. Turn any negatives into positives: It will put you into a more approachable mind-set and avoid unnecessary attacks.

   Example: "I want there to be no mugs on my desk because I feel it's disrespectful if I have to clean it up" becomes "I feel respected when my space is left clean." "I shouldn't have to start my day cleaning up garbage" becomes "I am able to get on with my work immediately." "I don't hate everyone" becomes "I feel more generous toward my colleagues."

3. ***Find a neutral, private space to have the conversation***
Have the conversation in a place where both of you aren't going to feel under excess pressure—for example, less-than-ideal settings are in front of coworkers, in a very small room, or in a place where either of you feels defensive.

4. ***Starting the conversation***
State a value-neutral, fact-based description of the situation calmly. However riled up we may feel, it is crucial in these delicate moments to remove any overtly accusatory language.

Example: "When I come in every morning, there are a lot of coffee mugs and papers on my desk that are not mine." Do not say: "You leave all the mugs on my desk in the morning; it looks revolting, and I should not have to deal with this sh★t."

5. ***Say how it makes you feel***
Express your feelings. Do not qualify or apologize. Keep it simple. Inhale compassion and exhale anger. You dislike the activity of this person, not necessarily this person. It is unlikely the person is deliberately irritating (if they are, take comfort in the fact that they may have their own boundary issues and haven't yet found the courage to voice their issue with you). Sometimes we feel so defensive, we jump straight to attack mode.

Sharing the truth underneath that layer of armament—that it is really difficult for you to say this, or that you feel hurt or disrespected—humanizes the conversation. Remember, however, to maintain your agency (your power). It's not about how they "made" you feel. This is your boundary, your emotions, and your responsibility.

Example: "This is difficult for me to say, but I feel annoyed and disrespected when I see mugs left on my desk. For me, someone respecting my space means they respect me, and so I get angry when I see them there."

6. **State what you need in a clear and direct way**

Example: "I want to come in to a clean desk every morning and I would like it if you cleaned up anything you put there on the night shift before you go home."

7. **State what this would give you**

Example: "This would let me get straight to work in the morning without delay. I value our relationship, and this would help me work alongside you better too."

8. **State the consequences of breaking this boundary**

Example: "I want to give you fair warning that this is important to me, and, if it happens again, I will ask to be moved."

You want to give the other person a chance to honor your feelings, but you also want to show you are serious. Once a boundary is set, it is important to enforce the consequences of a boundary being broken—follow words with actions. It may feel extreme, but it shows self-respect.

Dealing with Difficult Reactions

Remember to set boundaries with love—limits are there to allow relationships to flourish, after all. A lot of the time, people don't realize the impact of their actions. If the boundary infraction has been going on for some time and you have not spoken up, then this may be a shock for the person listening.

Sometimes setting up a boundary may see the other person get defensive, angry, or questioning. Though they are entitled to their anger, you are entitled to your boundary. Do not mirror their response or be intimidated by it; instead, simply restate your boundary calmly, without capitulating or attending to their arguments. Signal that this is not a negotiation but rather the limit of what you find acceptable. Holding your ground calmly demonstrates that anger will not scare you into changing your mind.

Generally, boundary-setting conversations tend to happen on an ad hoc basis, i.e., when boundaries are crossed. Expressly communicating them can be anxiety-inducing, but setting and maintaining boundaries and learning how to handle people who fail to respect them gets easier and helps you protect your self-esteem.

Owning Your Part

Everyone's keen to brag about their relationships when things are going smoothly. Instagram is full of kissing couples, cozy beach snaps, and #besties. Less popular is taking a share of responsibility when things get messy. Then, in the privacy of WhatsApp or behind closed doors, tempers flare, events are dissected, and accountability is tossed like a hot potato. You'll usually hear blame ("You're wrong"), victimhood ("Why do you always do this to me?"), or shame (nothing at all—shame gets off on silence, disconnection, and withdrawal). It's natural to find yourself in one of these emotional garbage cans when things don't go well. Upon noticing, though, it's wise to get yourself the hell out of there. Blame, shame, and victimhood are all enemies of intimacy. They are blinding and suffocating forces, robbing us of insight, personal power, and connection.

That doesn't mean disagreements won't happen. Relationships that exist without any conflict are not relationships, merely two people who occasionally exist side by side. Close contact between two things generates friction. That's okay. This friction, or conflict, by which I mean anything from disagreement to a full-on verbal fight, is a natural and necessary part of intimacy and personal growth, yet we run from it as if it's a threat to ourselves and our connections. It doesn't have to be that way. The way we approach conflicts can make our relationships stronger. It's like *Super Mario Land* on Game Boy; we're navigating through a series of fights and challenges that allow the relationship to move up a level.

Conflicts within relationships mainly result in disconnection for one reason: People refuse, either consciously or unconsciously, to take responsibility for how they contributed to the situation in question. As relationships are cocreated between two or more people, so, too, is the conflict that's sometimes generated within them. The root of the word conflict comes from Latin, *con* (with) and *fligere* (to strike)—or to strike together. My point is that there is always a part that you will have played to contribute to the current situation— even unintentionally, or by omission. Perhaps it was by not saying something or not doing something, making an assumption, breaking an unstated boundary, or being unclear, but if it happened in a relationship, there is a place you can take responsibility too. Owning your part is not about right or wrong or about fault; it's about accountability. It's saying, "Yes, I did that and I can see now how *that* may have led to *that*."

This is important because unless both people can own their part in the discord, it's hard for either side to offer or receive a true apology—to cultivate forgiveness and move the relationship forward. Without this willingness to examine what went wrong, how all parties coconspired to create it, and a clear commitment to handling circumstances differently, it's hard for trust to be rebuilt.

This, like most things, is easier said than done. Sometimes, a sense of stubbornness and misplaced pride means we refuse to take responsibility for our part in the drama unless the person we're in conflict with takes responsibility for theirs. This is not only childish, but it denies us the benefits of taking responsibility, which are available whether or not the other person decides to join in the fun.

By owning your part, the first advantage you get to pile on your personal-development plate is power. Admitting you either chose or caused a situation, at least in part, means you're back in the driver's seat of your own life. You're recognizing that you have power and that chaos is not just randomly happening all around you without you (subconsciously) sanctioning it! Being able to meet someone as a responsible adult is an incredibly important part of having a relationship—the counterposition meaning that any interactions are simply coming *at* you and happening *to* you, rather than *with* you. It leaves you left to navigate a power dynamic rather than a relationship.

Second, investigating how you could have contributed to a set of circumstances and seeing how something you did created a result you didn't like will provide you with helpful self-knowledge. Conflict is wonderful for providing insight into our own blind spots—things that other people know about us but that we don't know about ourselves. This can be uncomfortable—discovering that we display arrogance or that we frequently mislead people is not an easy process. We've hidden these traits from ourselves for a reason, after all—we don't want to see what's there! Claiming these "secret," abandoned parts of ourselves is actually the loving thing to do, however. It allows us to develop self-respect and gives us a better chance of maintaining deeper connections because we can now truly bring all parts of ourselves into a relationship. Plus, more generally, we're less likely to go around unintentionally flinging unclaimed parts of our personality everywhere, which, I promise, as someone who's discovered pockets of arrogance, disdain, superiority, and collusion in her own abandoned soul suitcase, benefits no one.

> We are far more likely to hold people responsible for negative actions than positive ones, giving them credit or praise. Essentially, the worse the action, the more likely we are to think that the person intended for it to happen, rather than it being unfortunate, or mere bad luck. We think of blame and praise as being two sides of the same coin, but they really aren't. They are actually completely different processes in the brain; blame sees activity in the amygdala—the emotional part of the brain—whereas praise or credit is assigned in a more logical part of the brain. Just something to watch out for—especially if you're on a jury.[15]

These (free!) personal-development delights are available to you whether the other person wants to own their part or not. Something funny happens when you go and make yourself vulnerable in this way, though. Suddenly, as you admit what you did, everything softens, and they can see their part too. Even more magically, they are also willing to own up to it.

Swallowing your ego is a bit like when you drink a cup of baking soda and warm water for a stomach ache: It's initially deeply unpleasant and makes you feel a bit sick, but you feel so much better afterward. Promise. As Raylan Givens says in the TV series *Justified*: "If you run into an asshole in the morning, you ran into an asshole. If you run into assholes all day, you're the asshole." If there's one thing owning your part helps with, it's being less of an asshole. And when you've indulged in some asshole behavior, admit it, learn from it, and love yourself anyway.

How to Give a Good Apology

The most healing kind of apology to both give and receive is one where someone doesn't just say they are sorry, but explains *why* they are sorry. The more specific someone can be, the better. It allows the person receiving it to feel heard and felt and both parties to move on from the event with some resolution from the situation. For example:

> "I'm sorry for raising my voice the way I did. I can see how that wasn't easy for you, that it didn't help me get my point across, and why your feelings are now hurt."

It can be humbling to do this, but it's also incredibly freeing.

Getting Off Your High Horse

Being on my high horse has been my favorite way to absolve myself of accountability. The ease of putting all the responsibility on someone else, before riding off, morally righteous, into a sunset of blissful impotence, is wonderfully satisfying to my ego.

Though being astride your high horse might give you a feeling of immense power and righteousness, paradoxically, due to the very nature of the beast, it means you are simultaneously declaring yourself a helpless victim.

My high horse is called Veronica. She is particularly vocal when it comes to men and is rather dominant when first dates go poorly. When it comes to disagreements with coworkers, family or partners, she casts herself in a saintly hue, all the while heaping blame on others. She loves contradictions too. I think the most absurd story I've heard her tell is that all my dates were going badly because I was too strong and powerful. "Isn't it awful that all men are so intimidated by beauty and talent? Poor me, there's nothing I can do . . ." was her favorite story for a while. You can always tell when someone is on their high horse—they speak of being wronged, but they make very strange-looking victims.

My wonderful friends call me out when Veronica's around because, although they love my headstrong side, they also know it doesn't serve me or the situation well. There are two reasons I am able to get off my high horse when my friends call me out. The first is that I gave my horse a name so I don't identify it with my true self anymore—it's a pattern, not me—and therefore letting go of "having to be right" is that much easier if they talk about Veronica, rather than Felicity. The second is that I can feel how much they love me, and they will give me attention and hear me out whether I'm distressed because I'm morally right or because I made a mistake. One of the payoffs for sharing a story where you are dramatically wronged is receiving sympathy and attention. If I know I am going to receive that anyway, then the motivation for me to continue with my victim story is less compelling. They have been there through enough f★★k-ups of my own contriving—I know now that they will love me regardless.

I'm glad I have friends that can help me down from my high horse with love, excruciating though it is sometimes. Being right is very comforting, but, in the long term, it's likely to be the only sop you're left with. Being on your high horse is a swift route to loneliness and misery. It has a short shelf life with most people, and it can make you behave like a demanding toddler.

Someone refusing to come off their high horse is so afraid of failure, rejection, and being wrong that they can only tolerate acquiescence to their point of view. Even if the person who challenges their version of events isn't the same individual who is initially believed to have wronged them, they often will not allow their powerfully stated victimhood to be disputed. In fact, daring to dispute their version of events can sometimes have them ride higher, as you, too, become part of their proof that they are indeed wronged, since you refused to take them seriously!

When someone regularly engages in this kind of victimhood, they tend to try to find someone else who is astride a victimhood high horse about the same thing, whom they can prance around in ever-decreasing circles. This is called collusion. I'm somewhat embarrassed to say I used to do this. A lot. In fact, I set up my social circle in such a way that I knew particular friends would collude with me on certain things, and I could go to people accordingly, depending on whatever it was I wanted sympathy for.

If I was having a problem with my boss, I'd call the friend who I knew would let me play moral superior there, because she had similar issues with her manager. If I wanted to rant about dating, I'd message a friend who I knew would back up my story that my lack of success had nothing to do with me but rather everyone else.

If you recognize yourself here—if you've colluded or sought collusion—stop it; it's not kind and it's not helpful. Being on a high horse keeps the rider a prisoner of a place they don't like. It enables someone to keep doing the same thing over and over, even though it's giving them undesirable results. It keeps them stuck in a mind-set where they tell themselves they have no power over their own life or relationships. You're confirming a story that hurts— either them or you. If you're on your high horse, it's time to dismount, meet someone face to face, one human being to another, and reconnect on more equal footing.

Victimhood

When we adopt a victim "mentality," we *perceive* whatever is happening in our life as occurring through forces beyond our control. Despite being at the center of the drama, we absolve ourselves of all responsibility and insist we have no power to change anything. In victimhood, all focus is on the powerlessness of the wounded self, a kind of "life is pain" attitude. *Victimhood* may display itself as resignation, a kind of sad stoicism, or woeful helplessness.

I'm using the word "victimhood" instead of "victim," because a victim is someone who is genuinely harmed and adversely affected by forces *outside their control*. For them the term "victim" is not a mind-set; it's a statement of reality. Victimhood, meanwhile, is when someone has adopted a perception of the world where they are *always* a victim; it's their general outlook rather than confined to a temporary event. You can certainly be a victim of something; you cannot be, unconditionally, a victim. We are human beings: We are not prey and we are not enduringly powerless, even though it may sometimes feel that way.

Someone who is trapped in victimhood is likely to experience a lot of drama in their lives, which they believe has nothing to do with them. Rather, the turmoil is coming "at" them for no reason other than their own bad luck, a series of unfortunate things happening "to" them. The world can be unfair—and it is, frequently—but the important thing is what we do next. Someone in victimhood is stuck feeling disempowered; rather than able to captain their own existence, they are beset with problems. They cannot see that these problems could be in part a consequence of their own thoughts, actions, or feelings. They may seem dedicated to a pessimistic view of the world—at times it might even feel that they are getting off on being miserable.

If dealing with someone like this sounds draining, that's because it is. Regular conversations with someone in a victim mind-set feels like being assaulted with relentless negativity. On top of that, people who feel they have been wronged aren't always the most compassionate souls when it comes to letting a bit of attention and love flow the other way. A Stanford University study connected the feeling of being wronged with behaving less generously toward others.[16] When participants were asked to recall a time when they were treated unfairly, right before being asked to help others complete a simple task, they were more likely to refuse than another group of participants, who were asked to recall a time they were bored. The unlikable side effects of dealing with someone in victimhood aside, it's important not to slip into judgment yourself.

For a start, we all do this from time to time. When it comes to personal responsibility, or hauling ourselves out of a hole, sometimes we choose to dodge the uncomfortable bullet of doing the difficult, proactive thing and instead claim that we are powerless or matters are simply hopeless. More than once have I swooned on the sofa in victim mode, and a small degree of wallowing (I time myself now—I'm allowed to hide under the covers for a half-hour pretending that putting on weight, or someone postponing a meeting or criticizing me, is the worst thing ever) never injured anyone. We're allowed to have hurt feelings and attend to those. It might not be a big deal, you might know you'll get another job interview or date or that it's simply your ego that's sore, but it still feels rotten, and that's okay.

If you're a friend witnessing this, be careful and pay close attention. What might *look* like victimhood could be someone sinking into depression and needing proper mental health treatment. If someone is so high up in anxiety that they can't see the forest for the trees, and their body has gone into fight-or-flight response, that needs to be soothed with slow breathing, gentle attention, and calming words before any kind of conversation can take place.

Even if that's not the case, blame someone for "being a victim" and you are simply boxing them back into that mentality. (You're also getting on your high horse yourself.) People do not adopt this mind-set consciously, and often it is learned from childhood. Perhaps this was how they saw their mother and father talk about the world. Perhaps in their family they had to be sick, upset, or unfortunate before they were able to get genuine attention from their parents, be listened to, and have their needs met.

Victimhood may also be driven by anxiety—fear of failure, abandonment, or wrongdoing. Sometimes people feel that if they admit to a mistake, they risk losing the love and respect of their peers. They might believe people will leave them unless they make themselves so pitiful that others feel they have to stay. There are benefits to this "poor me" mind-set: It often means others actively avoid criticizing or upsetting you because you are already sad.

Some people feel that if they are the victim of misfortune, they can demand certain treatment or claim they have a "right" to certain things. People may struggle to assert themselves, cope with criticism, or ask for what they want based purely on their own intrinsic value as humans. This sounds like a damning diagnosis, but the reality is, we all find ourselves here from time to time. I've definitely pulled a few puppy-dog eyes in my life, or overdramatized a mildly uncomfortable situation to get the sympathy I want from friends—then convinced myself that is the reality. It reminds me of the "last brownie" game in the film *Notting Hill*—where each character has to paint their life's woes in such a pitiful hue that the diners feel sorry for them and give them the last piece of cake at supper. We all naturally step into victimhood at times; it just becomes damaging when we stay there—or we are less conscious of doing it and think we genuinely have no power.

For someone in whom victimhood is deeply entrenched, therapy will be the only long-term solution. However, if there is a specific situation with a friend, partner, or family member, these five steps have served to help me.

1. *Can you approach this with empathy?*
   If you don't feel like you have the patience, energy, or neutrality to communicate clearly and compassionately with the individual when they speak like this, it is better

to realize this, withdraw, and set up boundaries. Otherwise you risk fueling the fire and causing upset for both of you.

2. *Set up boundaries*

You are not obliged to help the person, solve their problems, or give them attention. Remember, your first responsibility is to yourself. Decide what you are willing or able to give and set up a boundary. For example, you might say: "Just to let you know, I can only listen for five minutes." Or perhaps: "I can hear you are hurt and upset, and I'm sorry about that. I actually have some things going on right now, and I'm not able to listen, but come back to me later when you are ready to talk solutions."

3. *Listen and repeat it back*

This is an active listening technique that helps reflect back to the person in victimhood how dramatic they might be behaving, as well as helping them feel heard, which is helpful if what they need is attention. For example, if they say, "I am fighting with my partner and it's just unbearable and the end of the world right now," you might respond: "Okay, so I understand: Your partner is angry at you, and it feels unbearable and like the world is ending—is that right?" Don't react; just stay very calm and repeat back what they are saying. Don't get drawn into offering solutions.

4. *Accept their version of events*

Don't challenge, but gently ask questions. Accept what is going on for them, that things are bad. Then ask, "So what do you want to do about that?" If they say, "I can't do anything," just accept that and say, "Okay, then. Guess there's nothing anyone can do." Take their version of events as it is; don't engage or try to get them to see it another way yet. You want them to focus on how they would like to respond to it. Other questions like "What would the most powerful version of yourself do in this situation?" can also help them think in ways that remove them from that mind-set. Or you might try, "In an ideal world, what would you do next?" You can even ask: "What's one thing you could do for yourself right now to feel better?" Then follow up with: "And how can you make that happen?"

5. *Invite them to make a change*

After they have identified one thing they might want to do to alleviate their negative feelings or move toward a solution, say you have an invitation for them and ask if they would like to hear it. You can say something like "My invitation to you would be for you to take this step forward right now—would you be willing to do that?" Whatever their answer is, accept it, and draw the conversation to a close. If their answer is no, you can say, "Okay, great, well, thanks for brainstorming all the same," or something that doesn't attempt to take responsibility for their change.

Remember to set your own boundaries. If someone is in victimhood and you want to help them out, empathy and listening go a long way. It doesn't mean you have to confirm their point of view is correct, but you can allow them to feel heard and don't try to "fix" them; that's not your responsibility and it just removes more agency from them. Be careful, too, that you don't leap into judgment or tell them to snap out of it. It's possible to be so fixated on not indulging victimhood that you ignore genuine issues that need resolution and attention from external sources. People can have legitimate complaints and need genuine support. It might be an employee raising a concern about a certain process in the company. Even if it isn't, remember that the person's pain is real for them, and perspective is hard to come by when you're upset. Frankly, when we're down an emotional hole, we often need a hand up to see that there is a way out—even (and perhaps especially) if it's a hole of our own making. Being an adult—rather than a wounded child—is not an easy switch to make. We all find ourselves regressing, and it's wise to remember that. Talking to someone in victimhood requires a great deal of patience and sensitivity as well as an acute alertness to whether there is a legitimate issue that needs listening and attending to, victim mentality or not.

Blame

Blame is an ugly little bridge troll that feeds our lack: lack of self-esteem, lack of trust, and lack of power. It acts based on our worst feelings and grows fat on our scarcity. Blame is cheap these days. They say sex sells, but it is fear and judgment that *really* make people spend money. Trust me, I've worked in newspapers. Blame-generated anger and petitions for punishment are the media's bread and butter. Politics really gets off on blame too.

Doesn't it make you mad? No wonder we're all so quick to do it. It's almost definitely all their fault the country is in the state it's in. They should be made to pay for their actions, shouldn't they?

And that's the thing about blame … it's so easy to fall into. Blame generates more blame, ping-ponging anger and hurt back and forth, making the emotional divide between us greater and greater, and moving further and further from the original issue.

It puts blinkers on us and makes a person the problem, rather than a situation. It is narrow-minded and seeks retribution rather than resolution. And so we get stuck in a blame cycle.

There are a few assumptions that drive blame. The first is this notion that we are always consciously able to choose our actions based on the outcome we want.

When we blame, we assume people could have anticipated the negative consequences of their actions. Despite being able to choose a different option, for some mysterious reason (we usually fill in the blanks here and say it's because they are a bad person), they did not do the "correct" thing.

The truth is, most of the time, people are doing the best they can with the hand of cards they are playing. It's just that we all start with a slightly different hand. Assume the person you're tempted to blame had a good reason for saying what they said or doing what they did. Their choices were either logical or hard to avoid, given their mind, unique set of beliefs, and history.

If you could slide perfectly into their shoes, their behavior wouldn't seem unreasonable. It's just a matter of vantage point and knowing what's occupying their vision, activating those thoughts and feelings, and directing their decisions at that time. Blame is really just a perspective problem.

This doesn't stop people from taking responsibility for their actions, but it should remove the layer of judgment that often comes with it. The castigation, accusation, and bullying that come with blame are usually unhelpful. Instead of passive-aggressive punishment, it's far easier to analyze the situation together, with an open attitude of acceptance. Posing questions that widen someone's perspective and empowering them, providing them with tools and knowledge so that they can choose more positively next time, is a more effective route—both in work and home relationships.

Simple Causes for Complex Events

When we blame, we assume that every event has a sole cause and that we must know what or who that is—and right away. Sometimes, there does seem to be an obvious trigger, but life is rarely that elementary. This desire to find a singular simple cause for complex occurrences is an attempt to stem the fear of losing control when faced with life's unknowable forces. However, blame is an ineffective tool for dealing with the uncertainty of existence.

Instead of trying to force things to be more mechanistic, pretending life can be predicted, we would be better off spending our time learning how to embrace uncertainty. So some things happened that we didn't expect or necessarily want—how can we see that as an opportunity? Could it be that these situations are a perfect place to test our self-belief and self-confidence and reaffirm that we are okay not always knowing? Perhaps we can use these moments to learn more—to go to the heart of matters and really pick apart what made things go wrong. It's great that we don't know everything. It allows us to make discoveries.

If instead we cover up our discomfort with blame, it leads to scapegoating. We blame either an individual or a whole community, simply because we need for an event to have a human cause in order to feel in control.

Blame seeks to slice groups of people down the middle and put them in one of two categories: victim or perpetrator. It divides rather than unites. It isn't interested in solving problems or taking positive actions, only the hollow victory of victimhood or the agitation of anger. Anger is a bright and powerful flame that can be useful to initiate change, but it burns out fast. It's like driving your car in first gear only—it wrecks the engine. You can use anger to get things started, to fight against genuine injustice, but staying angry obscures, rather than illuminating a better way ahead.

Making a Mistake Versus Being a Mistake

The third and most damaging of all the blame beliefs is this final one, where we confuse someone f**king up with them being a f**k-up. I talked about this earlier in relation to our own self-care.

Say, for example, you order coffee, and the waitress, while pouring your drink, spills it on your laptop. If you're worried about the consequences of your computer possibly breaking, you slip into blame instead of just thinking "They spilled coffee." You may also make the judgment that they are clumsy or bad at their job. If you are feeling particularly fearful, you may label them "useless." I say fearful because these judgments are simply a bid to try to avoid feeling your own fear. If your laptop is ruined, what next? Will you get into trouble at work? Will it cost a lot of money? Can you afford it? Will the waitress help you pay for it? You're not actually angry; you're afraid. And so you condemn her, saying that this coffee spilling is a sign that she is worth less than you.

Angry blame is often fueled by fear. When someone is angry at you, when they are on the attack, see if you can hear the fear underneath it and what that fear needs. Then speak to that, rather than allowing the anger to hijack the conversation and direct your response. It's really easy to meet anger with anger, but this doesn't solve anything. Remember, blame is simply a reflection of someone's emotional state—it's not an accurate assessment of the situation, and you do not have to take it as such.

You do not have to tolerate people shouting or blaming you for things that aren't your fault. You can walk away or you can ask to be spoken to quietly. However, under some circumstances and if you feel able, you may want to try the tactic of treating the anger as fear. Imagine that the person full of resentment is simply telling you that they are scared. Keep calm, find out what they are afraid of, and soothe that fear first. It might be easier to find a solution.

Along with generating anger and negativity on both sides, the "blame" way of thinking rebounds negatively on our own self-worth. If an action with an undesirable outcome means something undesirable about the author of that event, it follows that we ourselves are not allowed to make mistakes without labeling ourselves as mistakes. Forget that as toddlers we learn to walk by falling over or learn about what is dangerous by hurting ourselves.

This incredibly self-restricting belief means that if we misjudge our own actions, we'll be forced either to go into denial when we f**k up, condemning us to continually repeat our patterns, or to hide in the shame cave (more on that next). It's just not true—making a mistake doesn't mean you are a mistake. You are more than what you do.

Shame

If blame is a bridge troll, shame is its toxic cave troll of a sibling. Shame lives in darkness and silence, alone, in the place where love goes to die, a frozen landscape.

Shame, like blame, is a defensive tool, and similarly one that, despite seeking to protect us from feeling pain or discomfort, often ends up causing more damage than whatever caused it in the first place. It's perhaps even more hurtful than blame, although it's a branch of self-blame, because it pollutes our entire world. Blame disconnects us from one person or group of people whom we think is wrong. Shame seeks to convince us not that we did something wrong, but that we *are* somehow wrong as human beings—and what's so awful about this conclusion is that we can't escape ourselves.

When we are afraid there is something wrong with us, we preemptively isolate and disconnect to avoid being rejected. We falsely believe that there is nothing we can do to change the situation—that the fundamental fault lies in our being. We hide our actions, parts of our characters, feelings, or experiences that we falsely believe are ugly, broken, or deformed, from everyone—even those close to us. Research professor Brené Brown says, "If you put shame in a Petri dish, it needs three things to grow exponentially: secrecy, silence, and judgment."[17]

Shame's love of isolation makes it dangerous—it means we cannot get the support we need to deal with whatever it is that caused the shame in the first place. Sharing and being heard are immensely healing. Shame is not really an emotion, but a frozen layer of ice hiding the hurt or whatever unacceptable emotion or attribute we feel is underneath it. In shrouding what we think lives under that shame—either from other people or even ourselves—we are really hiding those parts of ourselves that most need attention and care. It is like going to the doctor's for a checkup and chatting about your cold, but failing to tell him about a massive bullet wound in your back and hoping he doesn't notice.

There are some people that think shame is useful for keeping our behavior in line, for stopping society from running ragged, for making us good people. I don't agree. There is a lot of shame in this world. If it really worked like that, we wouldn't have the problems we do. Shame doesn't stop problems; it just stops us from getting help. Worse still, those suffering with very high levels of shame won't seek help until total annihilation is on the horizon. Anyone on a self-destructive path doesn't just sabotage their own life; they impact others as they spiral downward. We are all deeply connected as humans, perhaps more than we realize. Whenever we reject or disconnect from someone, there are two or more people that get hurt—the one pushing away and the one pushed away.

Shame, because it makes us assume people hate us, is highly destructive. It's associated with eating disorders, social phobias, addictions, anger, and rage. We don't feel able to talk about our experiences, and we feel unable to correct them—after all, we are the problem. This leaves a lot of emotional energy nowhere to go, and many people suffering with shame will channel it into toxic behavior, all the while anticipating that the same fault that caused the initial undesired behavior will bring failure again.

Shame makes us so darkly inward-staring we don't even realize that there are other people in shame's cave with us, in the exact same situation, feeling the exact same thing. Shame is so deeply preoccupying that it makes it hard for us to empathize with others—it makes us forget we are human, that we are fallible, that, frankly, we are made to f★★k up. We're so busy focusing on how wrong we are as individuals, we can't see all the other mitigating factors that influenced the situation, or other people that might have played a part. We assume we are omnipotently wrong.

It is empathy, in the end, that saves us from shame. Where shame makes us believe we are different, recognizing our humanity helps us realize we are the same. If we can talk to others about our experiences, and be listened to with kindness and acceptance, we begin to remove that freezing layer from our souls so we can actually feel the grief or fear or pain, express it, and then look at what needs to be done to move forward.

One major fact that must truly be felt if anyone is to recover from shame is that just because we take part in some hurtful behavior, we are wrong. It doesn't define us permanently: it's not our true nature. This doesn't stop us from taking responsibility for our actions—far from it. It is shame itself that prevents us from being responsible, because we've been wrongly assuming that we are somehow uniquely flawed, with an abscess on our character we can't remove, rather than that we simply made a mistake. When we unhitch what we do or have done from who we are or can be, we are given some space to breathe. We can express remorse, look at ways to mend or clean up the messes we have made, and, over time and with support, trust in our own worthiness and ability to handle the situation in the future. We can take the right levels of responsibility without crumbling into self-loathing and hiding away in isolation.

This idea that we are not defined by our actions may be hard for some to swallow. We love labels in our society—if we steal, we are a thief; if someone says something nasty, they must be a bully; if we betray someone, we are a rat; and if we say a sexist thing, we must be a sexist. Then we infuse all these labels with so much pungent revulsion that it's almost as if being called one writes us off as humans for life. People make mistakes. We are undeniably more than what we do. Our value can't be defined by our job, our salary, how many marathons we run, how many cities we've visited, how many people like us, or how many kids we have.

Your life is not a series of doings but a journey of becoming. You may learn how to become through doing, but it's not a straight road. You actually need to do it wrong if you want to get it right. Mistakes are how you learn. F**k up or you're totally f**ked. Don't you just love this spiritual stuff?

Coming out of the shame cave

Think of an experience you feel some shame over. Call it into your mind, and breathe into your belly. Be soft with yourself. Remind yourself: "I am a fallible human; my value is no less or no more than anyone else's." Now it is time to melt the ice, express what you feel, and tell the situation as it is. You can write it down, record a selfie video, or, if both of these feel too much, put your headphones in, play some loud music, and say it out loud, either somewhere private or in front of a mirror. After you've done this, ask yourself, "How might this be not just about me?"

Honesty

Hiding from honesty is the quickest route to loneliness I know. An unwillingness to say or hear what's real means life becomes devoid of intimacy. Lying about your feelings is the emotional equivalent of shutting a door in someone's face. Both sides lose out on a chance for genuine connection, and the only relationship you have is one with your own fantastical perception.

That doesn't mean being truthful or hearing someone express honest emotion is easy, feels comfortable, or looks good. The reward for honesty might be love and connection, but arriving in that place is a process requiring humility, practice, and a few f**k-ups. It requires trust in the power of vulnerability over self-doubt, worry, imperfection, and rejection. Honesty is a dialogue and its main aim is intimacy; it is not, as some would have it, about causing offense as you walk away from someone, blaming the other for being too sensitive while crying "it's a free country."

The intention of honest communication is important. It is not sharing controversial opinions for no reason other than the joy of broadcasting or feeling your impact—that's attention-seeking entitlement. Honesty is not an excuse to offload your unprocessed emotional gunk onto other people, simply because you have a mouth, phone, or keyboard and you can. It requires you to take responsibility for your feelings even while you share them: They are your emotions and opinions and ultimately the onus is on you to handle them. It asks you to speak not only truthfully but in such a way that people can hear your communication—phrasing yourself so that your meaning isn't masked by provocation or unnecessary upset. If that requires you to step back for a minute and find out how to say what it is you need to, then so be it. It does not always need to be impulsive.

So often, truth-telling isn't seen as something that may allow us to get closer if we stick around and seek understanding but is instead treated as a dangerous weapon, a kind of emotion-laden medieval mace, wielded about in times of trouble. It feels so threatening we only use it when there's nothing to lose, when the time has passed for amends to be made successfully. We only really tell our boss the issues we faced at work during the exit interview. We finally share with our partner all those things that annoyed us and what we really wanted during sex, as we break up.

Sometimes, we hang onto our truth for fear or shame, and only release it when we've totally lost control—say in an argument—but often our honesty becomes so smothered in blame, bile, and defensiveness that any nugget of authenticity gets lost. Then we end up apologizing for what we said and discounting it, though it's actually just the delivery that was off.

Other times we smuggle truth into an angry confrontation because, although our souls demand that we say it, we don't know how to find the space and we are nervous about how it will be received. We are being sneaky. We know in an argument it's less likely to be heard—that emotions are so high, it will just get lost in the melee of sensation. We pretend to ourselves that we are giving honesty without truly imparting it.

Honesty is not a weapon; it's a catalyst. Sure, it can be volatile. But just as fire can be destructive, in the right hands it can also be purifying. Honesty puts the heat of our attention onto a particular situation, emotion, or issue. This heat has the capacity to change the shape of whatever it comes into contact with. Humans naturally fear change, but that doesn't mean it's always bad. Just as glassblowers work with molten glass under intense temperatures, or goldsmiths plunge the gold into the hottest part of the fire in order to mold it, honesty provides the heat to alchemize our relationships from base elements into something beautiful.

The Honesty Cycle

At its core, honesty is pure love. It asks us to reach into our hearts and attend to what's there with all the humility and grace we can muster. We will see parts of ourselves we want to hide from and uncover feelings we'd prefer not to feel. Yet honesty demands we move toward these heart cracks like valiant mountaineers. This is the first stage: being truthful with ourselves.

The second stage is living in accordance with these truths, attending to what is there, and sharing the pain, fear, and hurt as well as the happiness, desire, and longing with the humans around us. To be honest with another about what lives in our hearts is to take on terror—to face down the fear of loss, abandonment, rejection, rage. It means sacrificing fantasy and risking reality—choosing the anarchic electricity of life over the comfort of sunny, syrupy romance. It does not always need to be the bad stuff either—honesty is as much happy loving truths as the ones that might be perceived negatively. Remember, though—not everyone wants honesty. If you feel that might be the case, ask if someone is willing to hear, and respect their reply. This is not about violating people with "your truth."

The third stage of this honesty cycle is being willing to hear another person's honesty, to listen and receive the truth with an open heart. Hearing honesty can be as hard as being honest, but it is necessary—it helps us to practice love and acceptance, both for ourselves and others. Often our reaction to others' honesty takes us back into our own selves, where we can uncover more truths about our character. Practicing this honesty cycle with those we love refines and polishes our character, bringing our dark and light sides into play, generating self-knowledge, acceptance, and intimacy.

Yet honesty is so taboo that we don't often get to experience this—instead, we mollify and pacify, sharing only the palatable half and burying the important part. Or we simply lie.

Mostly this is due to fear, shame, lack of trust, or disrespect. However, we convince ourselves it's because we don't want to make anyone uncomfortable or be socially inappropriate. We don't only lie to ourselves and others; we lie to ourselves and others about why we lie to ourselves and others.

Remember, there's a difference between harm and hurt— harm is pointless and destructive. Hurt is inevitable and recoverable and can lead to growth and reconciliation. It hurts when you have an operation—even if that operation goes on to save your life. Honesty can cause hurt—but it shouldn't cause harm.

Demonize or Patronize? What You're Choosing to Do When You Lie

Language is already layers on top of experience. Even when we aim to tell the truth, misunderstandings happen.

When you know what feels honest for you and instead you choose another route—silence, half-truth, or deception—you dishonor yourself, your relationship, and the other person.

Why are you lying? Perhaps there's an assumption that the other person can't handle your honesty—that your truth would be too much, or they would not be strong enough to handle it. Either way, you're demonizing yourself or patronizing someone else. Underneath that, you feed a belief that you'll be rejected if you truly share who you are or what you think.

It's not true. Sure, from time to time some people will find honesty hard to handle. Tell the truth and some may temporarily or permanently disconnect from you. Not everyone, though. And far fewer than you might imagine. People respect honesty, and strong relationships do survive. The only way you discover this is by putting it to the test.

Lying is cruel for two other reasons. The first that, by constantly only telling half the truth of your emotional reality, you lose touch with your own feelings—you hide yourself from someone else, only to buy into your own lie. How are you treating yourself if even your own emotions aren't allowed?

Another unkind side effect of lying is that if someone senses that something is going on for you and asks, only for you to lie and pretend everything is fine, then you are contributing to them thinking their perception is off too. People instinctively know what's true—when you don't tell them, they either think they are going crazy or assume the truth is something much worse, which is why you don't want to share it. Your lies can infect someone else's reality.

But what about those people who seemingly don't want to hear an uncomfortable truth? I myself have struggled more than once to receive some, ahem, perceived criticism, even while recognizing the courage it would have taken, as a friend, to share it with me. If you want to be honest with someone but you are concerned it could have an impact on their feelings, or it might be hard for them to hear it, ask yourself these four questions first:

1. *Do they already know?*

If you believe your friend or partner is already aware of the reality, then you may want to offer your love, support, and a space to talk, rather than simply imparting facts, or letting them know that you've also noticed, which is likely to just make them feel worse. For example, if you're concerned about a change in a friend's behavior, be that eating, drinking, working, or going out, they will very likely be aware of the changes themselves and realize that they are masking a deeper problem. Simply saying, "We think you are eating/drinking/partying/working/shouting too much" is unlikely to be received well. It's up to them whether they choose to accept help or not.

2. *Why are you telling them?*

There is only one reason that flies here—to build a deeper, more connected relationship. Discharging a load of so-called honesty (whether it's true or not) to make yourself feel better or put them in their place is not going to build intimacy, because it's a personal attack for selfish reasons—a game that only has one winner. We all get angry and honest sometimes, and it's not the end of the world or even your relationship if this happens, but it might not be the best way to communicate your concerns.

3. *How are you telling them?*

If this is a particularly emotionally charged topic for you, it might be a good idea to remove all blame from it. Write down what you want to say or scribble out all your emotions on a piece of paper first. One time when I was leaving a job, I wanted to tell the truth but I didn't want it to come out of my mouth in a string of angry venom, so I wrote my own run-through resignation letter first, so I could leave without resentment.

4. *Ask them*

If you've checked in with each of these questions and believe your motives are good, it's okay to prepare your friend/family member/coworker with some words that allow them to tell you whether they want to receive your honesty or not. For example, "There's something I want to tell you, but it's hard for me to say and it might be hard for you to hear—would it be okay if I told you now?" You could also offer to text them later or tell them over the phone.

Little Lies and Lying by Omission

Some people think telling white lies is acceptable—that small amounts of dishonesty in certain situations is, in fact, far more moral than ruthless honesty. Some people think that by leaving certain facts out they aren't lying—even though the takeaway from the situation is significantly altered.

There's a good argument to be made in favor of kindness—and sparing someone's feelings when they aren't seeking truth but merely reassurance or approval. Sometimes we ask, "Does my butt look big in this?" when really we mean, "I don't feel attractive today—can you help me feel confident?" Or we ask, "Do you like the meal I made?" when we really mean, "I hope you can feel my love—can you?" We aren't perfect beings, and if you can hear the more truthful request behind the words themselves, you might want to answer that instead.

Sometimes, however, asking for honest feedback when you just want to be acknowledged or praised is a hard habit to break—and it's usually broken when you repeatedly get what you ask for and it feels bad. I know this one—I used to send friends copies of articles I'd written and ask: "What do you think of this?" when I really wanted to hear what they liked about it, what they agreed with in it, and to feel good that they had read my piece. I soon realized, after I received some genuine warts-and-all feedback, that genuine feedback was definitely not what I was after. Now, if I just want praise, I ask specifically what people like about it. Fundamentally, though, what someone else thinks—honest opinion or not— is never more important than our own sense of worth.

The question of whether to tell the truth or not depends on intention. If you are holding back some information from someone, despite honesty benefiting neither them nor your connection in the long run, then you are scared of the small demands on your honesty for the same reason you shiver at the big challenges. It's best to be flexible around this: You don't need to whack someone with a bunch of honesty if they're already struggling at the end of a long day—it's going to be hard for them to hear you then.

Being truthful in small places, even when it's uncomfortable, can help us build the communication skills necessary for those big moments of honesty. It allows us to practice being assertive. It reveals how strong both we and our relationships are—that we can experience disagreement and the overcoming of small conflicts and criticism ("I hate it when you put the couch cushions on the floor" or "I really don't like that thing you do in bed" might be one example) and survive anyway. I also think that when we engage in white lies or hold back a key truth, we miss out on those moments of unconditional love. We forget that we don't have to like everything about each other to still fundamentally trust, love, and enjoy connecting with someone else.

Lying Recap

Think of the last time you told a lie—or failed to really share the truth about what you thought or felt. Why did you do that? What was the belief about yourself, the other person, or your relationship that made you do it? Ask yourself if continuing to act in line with that belief is beneficial or painful to you. What is the impact of acting like this on those around you?

Being Unconditional

Every year, millions of people stand tremulously in front of friends and family and promise to love their partners "for better, for worse, for richer, for poorer, in sickness and in health ... till death us do part."

This promise, written into Christian marriage rites, is a simple ideal of unconditionality that for many of us is at the heart of what we believe about love.

Yet being unconditional is alien to our everyday lives—we might glimpse this kind of love with a pet or with a child, but most of us have lost touch with how to be unconditional in the way we express ourselves with others. For all the many people who get married every year, around half also get divorced. Marriage is a hard practice, and unless we are specifically religious, we're not offered much in the way of guidance or example. But even God has conditions for entry to heaven, right?

Living in such a highly transactional culture, being unconditional has become a kind of mystical moonshine, a beautiful concept but inaccessible to the Earth dweller—too far from our lived experience. There is nothing inherently wrong with being transactional; conditional exchange, some argue, is a foundational element of society, established to manage and limit any inclination to act in ways that serve ourselves best.

Political philosopher Thomas Hobbes argued that the natural state of man was a state of war; we need social structures, which rely on law, the rights of property, and fair exchange. Without these, our lives would be, as Hobbes famously quipped, "solitary, poor, nasty, brutish, and short."[18] We might stick up our noses at his cynicism, but we still lock our doors at night and check our change as we exit the supermarket. Essentially, putting conditions on things works very well in some areas of our society—for the legal system, in shops, for mortgages.

However, living without some level of unconditionality in relationships—being unable or unwilling to give or receive unconditionally from others—is a slow death for our souls. It's also practically impossible, not to mention exhausting, continually tallying up what we owe or are owed by those closest to us. If we keep score of who last bought the milk or took the garbage out, how can we remember who loved first last time, who allowed themselves to be vulnerable first, or who forgave first?

This Is Life Too

"Unconditional" literally means without conditions: without qualifying, or providing a caveat. It means completely and totally committing your assets, be they your time, your trust, or the investment of emotional energy, trusting that these gifts won't be appreciated or returned.

It is saying "yes *and*" rather than "yes *but*" (that's a trick for people who love going to improv classes). It allows, accepts, and embraces rather than restricts, disputes, and grips. When it comes to love, it's the warm, pink marshmallow cloud we all want to bathe in, first from our parents, if we're lucky, then from our spouse, and then, perhaps, from our children.

If I aim to be unconditional in how I relate to my life, this means accepting, enjoying, and being grateful for everything that comes into my experience, whether I want it or I don't. It's a conscious choice to enjoy life whatever the circumstances— not just based on the "right" conditions (which, ironically, do not exist anyway). It's a contract with myself to seek pleasure and appreciation even in the most unlikely places, or adverse situations.

It means asking myself, "How can I enjoy this?" when the train is packed on the way to work and there's sweat dripping down the back of my new shirt. (It's hot. I feel alive. I'm grateful for my body working to cool me down.)

This embrace of life means that when my date cancels, and I'm all dressed up with nowhere to go, I'm willing to ask, "How I can turn this around?" (Seeing which friends are around to meet up, noticing that I am disappointed but it's not the end of the world, taking photos of myself looking pretty.) It means knowing that delicious juice can be squeezed from the ugliest fruit—and not ignoring, resisting, or rejecting the parts of life that, just for me personally, are harder to appreciate. It's an attitude that is constantly reminding me "this is life too"—that rain and storms are just as much part of existence as warmth and sunshine.

Learning to welcome and appreciate both the ups and the downs as equally necessary is our job, providing the balance and variety that makes life both challenging and beautiful.

Being unconditional with myself means adopting this practice at an even deeper level. From birth, many of us have learned (largely unconsciously) to divide ourselves into two: good and bad, acceptable and unacceptable, successful and unsuccessful, lovable and unlovable.

While these demarcations might be useful for functioning in society (it might be "good" not to steal something or espouse racist views, for example), it's not a great way to relate to yourself.

Underneath these labels, I seek to embrace all sides and parts of me. I choose to love myself regardless—if I fail, if I get fat, if I f★★k up, I won't reject myself. It is what it is, life is now, and I will not put conditions on my happiness or love for myself.

That's challenging for most people. We tend to think that punishing ourselves results in positive change—if we beat ourselves up enough about our bodies, our work, our faults, we'll be magically motivated to lose weight, gain muscle, earn millions, and be generous.

We also think we prefer people who are modest, who sell themselves short, or say they know nothing. A note on "humility" here. Humility is not insecurity or inadequacy or repeatedly resolving to do better, or putting down what we do have. Humility is actually the ability to listen better, to hear what's true and what's just noise or fear. It's the ability to see better, rather than looking through a lens that only allows you to see what is good in you and what is bad in others. Perhaps you wear the other set of contact lenses—the ones where you see only what is bad in you, and what is good in others. Humility allows us to see both, simultaneously, and make lots of Venn diagrams. It helps us to notice what we share with other human beings, even the ones we may initially dislike. That's one reason humility is such wonderful friends with unconditional love. Because it is concerned with what is, not what we would prefer, it allows you to stop focusing on the future for a minute and to see what's here right now.

Many of us today have very narrow ideas about who we need to be and what our life should look like before we're allowed to accept and enjoy them. That we need to be a certain weight or age to wear a certain dress, or speak a certain way to be on the radio. Perhaps we need to have a certain level of intelligence before we are qualified to write a book or be on TV—that only with a certain amount of a certain experience are we allowed to offer advice or opinions. It is a very common belief today that we need to have a specific amount of money or number of university degrees to qualify for the label "successful." Yet as a result of all these limitations on us as we try to live our "best life," we eventually feel antagonized when people who don't fit these arbitrary standards seem carefree, happy enough to wear the tight dress, write the book, start the podcast, and say they have a successful life.

Then, even when we hit the benchmark, we move the goalposts, so we never actually get the reward of the self-love we needed and promised ourselves we would feel when we started. Those places you don't want to love are actually the parts that need it most. If we approached food the way we treat our relationship to self-love, we'd only let ourselves eat when we weren't hungry, or have a sip of water when our thirst was quenched. It's nonsense. Love yourself anyway.

Cultivating a full and loving heart is very helpful when it comes to practicing unconditionality in relationships. Relating to people is hard; it's one of the most important components of our happiness, and we're not taught in any structured way how to do it. In all relationships, you'll need to accept and love yourself along the way, in all those places you are still conditional, transactional, and consumptive. One side effect of practicing being unconditional with yourself is that you naturally begin to generate a softer position toward others, realizing that most of the time, we are all doing the best we can, and we have more in common than we think.

All sounds too good to be true, right? Okay, so here's the catch. Life is conditional and humans are conditional: We all need food, water, and a whole host of other things to continue to survive. That's the challenge: How can we be unconditional in these very conditional bodies?

And what does that mean when it comes to relationships, which, as we all know, usually come with conditions too. (We might call them standards, or expectations—I prefer to call them boundaries, because they are there to keep us safe, not measure how we're falling short.) There are two ways of being unconditional that I'll discuss here: giving and receiving. They are two sides of the same coin, but there are slightly different challenges with each. But first: what being unconditional in relationships does *not* mean.

Being unconditional does not mean you give everything you have, even when you don't want to, just because you feel you should. This is people-pleasing, and it's a one-way ticket to resentment. Being unconditional does not mean you put up with things you dislike all the time or that hurt you. That's abandoning yourself and having poor boundaries. Being unconditional does not mean demanding everything another person has and expecting them to give it to you. This kind of behavior reflects an attitude of entitlement and it's a surefire way to make sure you're never satisfied.

Whenever we give or receive unconditionally, we create something that is of far more value than whatever service or object we are providing or accepting. From one heart to another, a little light stream of love is ignited. A connection that is based on abundance, gratitude, and compassion.

It does not depend on conditions being met and neither can the conditions be unmet, and so the beam cannot be broken. This cycle of loving reciprocity spools endlessly, a kind of revitalizing, regenerative energy. It is the kind of energy to endeavor to develop in a relationship with yourself, with life, and in your relationships with others.

Try this: Think of a place or a time where you felt restless, itchy, or dissatisfied. What conditions were you putting on that moment? Sit quietly now, and call it into memory. Try breathing in acceptance and love and letting go of expectations as you exhale. You could also try softly saying to yourself the mantra: "I expect nothing and appreciate everything."

Giving

You're probably familiar with the golden rule: "Do unto others as you would have them do unto you." It's a maxim that appears across many different cultures and religions, including the ancient civilizations of India, Greece, Rome and Persia, and is one of the main principles of Christian ethics (forming the bedrock of the teachings implicit in Jesus's Sermon on the Mount).

Unfortunately, this tenet has suffered a slight semantic shift over the past 2,000 years, one that changes the meaning entirely. For many of us, our relationship to giving has mutated from one that begins from a place of humility and love to one tied to expectation and demand: "Do unto others, so that they do unto you." A lot of us will only give to get, rather than giving for its own sake.

We pick up the phone and listen to our friend moan about their parents for ten minutes, so that we can moan about our parents for ten minutes afterward. When someone thanks us for helping them, we reply, "You would do the same for me"—a phrase that can sound more like a threat than a compliment.

In a business meeting we might promise, "You scratch my back and I'll scratch yours."

After work, we meet someone for a first date and buy them dinner. We offer to pay. If they let us foot the bill, we'll be asking ourselves out for coffee. That's how it works, right? The ones who refuse our money usually don't call back.

The relationship's good—until we say "I love you" and they don't respond in kind. Outrageous. How could one person love someone more than the other?! That would be insufferable. Unbearable. We demand fair amounts of love to be exchanged at all times. After all, we only give Christmas gifts to the people who treat us in return. And Secret Santa has a budget for a reason. Fairness is crucial.

Aside from this transactional *quid pro quo* approach to giving, we also frequently put conditions on our "gifts." Maybe we only give to people who we judge are deserving, people that we think have the "right" to receive gifts from us. For example, we might not give our sympathy to the rich man who suffers from poor mental health because "life is still easier for him." We won't give our money to a homeless person because "they would only spend it on drugs."

These are examples of conditional giving: when we will only give if the recipient seems worthy, or we offer on the basis that we receive something in return. We can do it consciously, knowing we definitely want something in return and we will be resentful if that thing doesn't come. Or we sometimes do it hopefully—we don't necessarily know if we will get anything in return, but that is our primary motivation: for example, if we act with generosity because we want to be liked or to look good. If we're Christian, perhaps we give because we want to get into heaven.

All of these conditional ways of giving, while understandable, limit us and the potential for our future relationships.

One of the reasons for this is that our choices in giving are often driven by a fear of lack; that there is not enough to go around and our stores will not replenish themselves.

It is difficult to acknowledge the flaw in the assumption that there is no joy in giving for giving's sake, that people will not help us unless they can expect something in return of equal or more value. It feeds into a worldview where we are only worth what we are able to give—only loved or valued for our skills, services, money, or possessions.

So, we instinctively cling to our resources, and spend our lives on the lookout for thieves or freeloaders, simultaneously trying to acquire more and more. If we buy into this philosophy, it means we ourselves don't ask for help because we feel as though we are a burden if we're unable to give anything in return. It means we don't trust people who give to us, because we are constantly waiting for the day of debt to arrive. We're forever forced to say "sorry" instead of "thank you." This perspective is deeply limiting, sentencing us to a depressing, mercenary existence.

Guilt Costs More Than You Think

There are other kinds of conditional giving at work in our lives too. One occurs when we give not to get something back, but because, if we don't, we feel bad. We give to negate the shame of choosing not to help. We do it even when we don't want to do it, and often with resentment (this gift's emotional "price tag"), because we feel we have to—we feel it is "owed" by us. We help our friend move even though we'd rather sleep in, or we go to our sister's graduation even though we find it boring and pointless. We give our neighbor a ride to the airport at 1 a.m. through gritted teeth; we may not like them that much, but we do it because it's expected and we'll feel guilty if we don't.

Dutiful or guilty giving is our way of avoiding the discomfort of learning how to give unconditionally. We give, even though we didn't want to, and we convince ourselves that this faux selflessness is enough to make us good people. In my mind, though, this giving is still transactional—we give to clear our consciences, or to avoid being seen as miserly or selfish.

I believe this kind of giving is the most toxic, because we disguise it as altruism, as being unconditional, but it hinders us in developing true generosity.

Giving on this basis often allows resentment to take root and fester within us; a resentment that we blame on the other person for asking. We then do the task mindlessly, ignoring the rising rancor (although this is often sensed by the receiver) instead of questioning our own feelings of scarcity or setting up a boundary to give only what we feel we can willingly, without resentment or expectation. It's fundamentally untruthful to the other person, and to ourselves, and stops us from ever experiencing the joy and freedom of unconditional giving.

Practicing unconditional giving is not about giving away everything you have. It's not about letting people take from you, or being obligated to say "yes" to everything. It's about knowing what you are comfortable to give without expecting anything in return. Of course, you might get a sense of warmth and strength and love for yourself and the receiver, but then again you might not.

Setting Your Terms

Establishing what feels acceptable in giving is hard for us to do initially. Start small. For example, say your friend wanted you to come and help her pack up to move over the weekend. It's your first weekend off for a while, and you want to be helpful, and you know it will be fun for an hour, but you don't want to give up your entire Saturday and Sunday for free. You have a few options. You could lie, and say you aren't around that weekend. The benefit of that is that it's easy to make something up and you don't run the risk of hurting your friend's feelings or feeling guilty. The cost, of course, is that you are lying, your friend might sense it, and you have to remember not to give yourself away while you upload that lazing-in-the-garden-with-a-spritzer selfie (#metime #sunnyafternoon #blessed) to Facebook. You could instead say "yes," try to make the weekend fun, and remember she owes you one when you move. Perhaps you go for an alternative option. You can either tell her you can do one hour at a certain time, as you want to relax that weekend, or you could stretch yourself a little and say you're around for two hours but you get to choose the playlist for the second hour.

There is something I have realized about myself: There is no price high enough to do anything that I can't make fun. I don't care about duty, obligation, shoulds, money—whatever I get in return. If it isn't fun, I don't enjoy it, and I can't make it so, then frankly life just feels too short and it's time for me to say "no." Sometimes this isn't even conscious—the universe just magically creates conditions that mean it is impossible for me to show up. I'm late, I forget, or I end up overbooking and having to cancel. This has happened so often that I've decided to stop trying to make myself do things I never felt like doing in the first place.

Letting Go of Crutches and Clutter

Giving unconditionally, for me, is fun. I find it both hugely freeing and revealing. In trying to give unconditionally, you get to see what you are attached to, what biases or behaviors you have adopted, your crutches, your clutter, the situations where you are scared to let go. However, it can be truly liberating to live this way. When you give unconditionally, you are telling yourself and everyone else, "I have a full, bountiful life, with no shortages; I have so much that I am willing to give things freely, with no expectation of anything in return. I am enough, and I have enough. I am secure. I am safe. I trust."

The secret that not everyone knows (we're too busy guarding our hoards and trying to snaffle what we can for free) is that giving actually makes you feel good. We are actually biologically built that way, because we evolved as cooperative animals, living in groups to survive. Professor Matthew D. Lieberman puts it best in his excellent book, *Social*:[19]

> Mammalian brains are wired to care for others and among primates this caring extends to at least some non-kin, even when there is no material return on the investment. Because of the way our brains are wired eating a piece of delicious cake is enjoyable whether we are hungry or not. Similarly, helping others feels good whether we expect something in return or not.

It may take some deep inner work, but at some point there will come a time when it doesn't feel like giving anymore, at least not giving in the same sense as you once understood it. Your love, attention, compassion and care, time, even physical belongings or money—the very act of giving them unconditionally reaps even more wealth. This kind of giving generates compassion, trust, and love. Think of the famed

Buddhist image of the candle: Even in relighting 1,000 more candles, the life of the candle is not shortened.

Your light and warmth are gifts from an infinite source; the choice to give unconditionally is the gift you give yourself and others at the same time. It also takes courage to say "no" and be true to yourself as you start, so that you can say "yes" to more and more in the long run.

Try to give a little bit more and more unconditionally. The best way to do this is in gradual increments that don't threaten your conditioned sense of fairness immediately; see if you can stretch yourself.

Receiving

Receiving, for many, feels deeply uncomfortable, whether accepting physical gifts, compliments, attention, or even love. The archetype of the receiver is not valued in many societies; instead, self-sufficiency is lauded, help is derided as a "handout," and the receiver is demonized as a "scrounger." It is seen as more powerful and soul-worthy to give than to receive. We operate this way, largely forgetting that for someone to give, there has to be someone receiving.

Nonetheless, we struggle on, trying to bargain our way through intimacy, believing everything must be paid back—if not financially, with physical objects, or our time, then emotionally, with effusive gratitude and ego-boosting compliments. Even in sex, if we receive pleasure, we feel we must return the "favor." Those times when we can't avoid receiving, then we devalue the gifts of others or simply try to rebuff them. "Oh, you like this dress on me? It's so old, and, look, I'm bursting out of it in the back. I actually think it's pretty ugly." This is the emotional equivalent of taking someone's Christmas present and, just as it touches your hands, crushing it, spitting on it, and tossing it back to them.

One of the teachers at the organization where I did my coaching program used to call this habit "discount jeans," based on our tendency to say "Oh, these jeans? I got them on sale" when we receive a compliment. We minimize the gift because receiving makes us vulnerable. Receiving can feel so destabilizing that often we panic in our inability to receive graciously and feel intensely awkward. Our egos demand we maintain a social image of plenty, of self-sufficiency; thus, bizarrely, a degree of wounded pride can be the consequence of a loving gift.

Sorry, Mom and Dad

Receiving requires humbly confronting the limits of what you can do or want to do and appreciating the existence of another and what they can offer. It means accepting graciously without resenting that you need their help (I'd just like to take this opportunity here to apologize to my parents, who have definitely had some resentment thrown their way because of my own insecurities). It sometimes means acknowledging that someone was able to provide something for you that you didn't even realize you wanted, needed, or would appreciate until it arrived.

The popular notion of giving and receiving sees the first as active and the latter as passive—and somehow that has come to mean submissive and less potent. However, the internal process of receiving unconditionally requires a huge shift of consciousness and a great inner strength and sense of self. It's just as active as giving, but in an invisible, felt way. It's not the same as simply getting, demanding, or taking. Receiving graciously requires us to actually open our hearts.

In receiving unconditionally, you make a declaration. You are telling both yourself and the giver: "I am consciously allowing you to provide for me something I could not do or get, did not want to do or get, or did not think about doing or getting for myself."

Everyone Has Something to Offer

Unconditional receiving asks us to confront our own conditioning and judgment too. It means not qualifying whom you will accept from or what form their love takes. It means knowing that, as a teacher, you can receive something of immense value from your student, even though they may have studied less. That the CEO can receive valuable insight from the man on the factory floor. It's believing, until it becomes knowing, that everyone has something to offer that is worth receiving, and it is important that we value and honor this by accepting it graciously. Is a few dollars from a poor man worth less than thousands from a billionaire? Allowing people to willingly give or serve is a statement of their value. Rejecting someone's unconditional offer because you perceive them or what they have to offer as less than you is ugly and narrow-minded. Sometimes accepting gifts can be hard, though, especially if the empath in us understands the kindness or self-sacrifice required to give the gift relative to the giver's situation. Could you accept change for the bus from someone who was homeless, willingly given, even if you needed the money to get home?

Occasionally, we put conditions on receiving because we think there is not enough, as in the example above. At other times, we are afraid to fully receive, because what is being given feels so good, bringing us a deep sense of warmth, gratification, and pleasure. We worry that, if we let in the good stuff, we are also opening ourselves up to experience pain when it ends. It's almost destabilizing. It's a bit like those times when you don't feel able to relax into your vacation because you know it's going to be over soon, even though below that fear you are craving to enjoy how great it feels in the moment. It's safer to refuse.

This vulnerability is amplified when we are receiving unconditionally. We feel that if we didn't "earn" it, it could definitely be taken away from us. That if we don't deserve it, we might have to give something away later to someone who angrily demands something to redress the balance.

We occasionally tip over into entitlement to try to avoid feeling these things, coming up with reasons why we deserve things to calm our anxious minds. Or we reject the gift altogether. It's crazy—we are so afraid of coping with change that we'd rather stay miserable than face a dynamic reality. If you had nothing and then you had something and then it changed and you have nothing again, you haven't really lost anything per se; you have just gained an experience.

We might try to block receiving, but we are receiving all the time. Believing you exist on a solitary plane where you are not constantly receiving is willful denial or a failure to see reality. Yet it's understandable. When we truly realize how much we have received, it's overwhelming. What have we done to deserve it? Well, maybe a few things, but we're still enormously in the red, and by that token there is nothing we can or could ever do to deserve all these gifts.

It's a false comparison. Your life, love, relationships, and value can't be processed like a bank balance. We're not talking about houses or clothes or vacations anymore. We're talking about human experiences, which simply can't be tallied in notes or numbers. Life is not about earning or deserving; it's about experiencing and becoming. The way you "pay it back" (it's really more of a case of honoring) is by fully receiving it: acknowledging it, experiencing it, leaning into the gift and the joy of it, and taking pleasure in it.

Here's an experiment: Try becoming a person who takes so much pleasure in receiving that you are a joy to give to. So often we scrunch our noses and crumple our shoulders awkwardly when we are given something, wracked with guilt and worried we don't deserve it. This ruins the experience for the giver as well. There's actually something beautiful in receiving even though we haven't earned it. It means people are giving you things because they *want* to give them to you. Because they love, respect, and admire you and it's fun for them to treat you. In "keeping score" or employing a tit-for-tat mentality, you fail to recognize the message with the gift: You are loved. That ought to feel good.

Giving, Receiving, and Redressing the Balance

Sometimes I think we should all just be a bit more dog. A happy dog doesn't care what it is that's being given— anything from a pat on the head to a bone is great—and it doesn't care why or who's giving it. It is simply joyful for the connection.

This is how we receive unconditionally: by accepting graciously something we haven't necessarily "earned" and enjoying it fully, because it's just so wonderful to be offered a gift in this way. By choosing to receive like this, we enable unconditional giving. Receiving unconditionally, we become part of something beautiful, an endless feedback loop of abundance and love. And by treating ourselves in this way, we realize we are beautiful and valuable no matter what we do. We didn't actually have to do anything to deserve it; we just had to be.

Receiving in this way is challenging, and it doesn't happen overnight. Plus, there are practical issues that arise—for example, if you want to receive something unconditionally, but you suspect someone else is giving it with strings attached. Of course, their strings are their responsibility (especially without a frank conversation—we aren't telepathic), but you still may feel awkward.

What if someone else gives me something and expects something in return? First things first, remember the strings are attached to the giver, not the receiver—they are their strings. So in one sense, that's not your problem.

However, there's also a slightly softer way of handling it. Juliette Karaman-van Schaardenburg, an empowerment coach, says, "If I feel the offer has strings attached, and my hesitation in accepting usually means there are some, I ask and it usually opens us up to much more connection and intimacy." You might say something like, "I'd love to receive this but I'm sensing there might be strings attached—is there anything you are expecting in return?" After all, you might be comfortable with the strings. It's nice to be kind here too; remember that none of us is perfect—in our receiving or our giving.

What if I don't want the thing being offered? Think about why you don't want it. Is there no use for it? Is it going to impact negatively on you in some way (e.g., your home is too small for it, etc.)? Will it make you feel uncomfortable? If so, a simple "No, thank you, but I really appreciate the gesture" will suffice and remind you that you are allowed to protect your boundaries. Another option, if they really want to give you something, is to tell them what they could give you instead: "Perhaps rather than going to the movies, we could take a walk and have a chat instead?"

What will happen if someone wants to give me something and I don't think they have enough? It's not your job to worry about that. It's your job to receive fully and with grace.

What if I want to give someone something unconditionally and they want to give me something in return for it? Well, you can tell them it's not necessary but, hey, why not just receive it gratefully? Someone is trying to give you a gift—enjoy it! Life is good!

Sex

I'm not always thrilled about having a feeling body as my home. Not only does it involve those tricky little wastrels called emotions, it also means being constantly interrupted by pressing physical demands (e.g., sleep, food, water, headache), which, paradoxically, I often find completely interfere with life. However, the big mother in the sky gave us a large compensation for living in a warm, fleshy, vibrational overcoat, and that, in my opinion, is good sex.

Good sex, or, for the sake of this section, the experience of pleasurable intimate physical connection between two or more consenting adults, is, for me and many others, one of the fundamental benefits of being alive. It usually involves genitals, but it doesn't have to: Ideally, you want your whole body and whole self involved. It definitely doesn't have to involve penetration or climax. Good sexual connection makes me feel healthier and improves my mood. There have been a number of studies of the benefits of regular sex, including stress relief, lower blood pressure, and improved immunity.[20]

Sounds great. So why aren't we all doing it more? Well, the good news is it has nothing to do with our sexual attractiveness or genital/digital dexterity; it has everything to do with fear, shame, and conditioning (three of the strongest antidotes to pleasure you'll ever find). I'm writing about sex from my perspective of being a woman with a vagina, but even if that's not you, hopefully this section will help you view sexual connection from a fresh perspective, inspire you to get more in touch with your sexuality, and maybe even try a few things at home.

Sexuality: aka Glorious Chaos

Sex can be one of the most dynamic and beautiful ways to enjoy being embodied in connection with another human being. The trouble is, it affects us so powerfully sometimes that we can find it destabilizing. Sexual energy is one of the few forces that can move us out of numbness and into feeling—and not just feeling, but feeling in connection. If we're not used to that, it can make us feel vulnerable and it can also bring to light things we usually ignore or aren't conscious of. This might look like fear: that we aren't good enough, or we're too much to handle, or that we will be abandoned. It might look like cultural conditioning ("If I have sex with her, she'll want a relationship, right?"). It might even be a surprising kink, or something that we find pleasurable but are also a bit embarrassed by. Sexual energy blows everything out of the closet. It leads to greater self-discovery and, in the long term, freedom—but it can be very difficult to confront. As well as showing the best of us, it also shows us the dark and primal side of our mind and our nature. Burying these feelings doesn't make them go away; it just gives them more power. Pouring light, love, and self-acceptance, as well as a genuine curiosity, can help. Remember, humanity is thousands of years old. There's nothing that you find sexually challenging that hasn't already been dealt with or experienced by many others.

Sometimes, because sex illuminates in this way, we assume it is dangerous, when really it's just a mirror powerful enough to show us what is going on in ourselves. Forget hips; it's genitals that won't lie. If they want it, they want it, and if we aren't feeling it in any way—maybe we don't feel safe or can't get our mind off a work project—well, they aren't getting off. You can't control pleasure and attraction, so of course religion, science, and culture have been cautious and clinical about them. Plus, sex makes everyone feel vulnerable. We need to talk and be open-minded with each other about it so that we have a chance at experiencing the kind of transformative pleasure, intimacy, and connection that sex can offer us. Face our fears without the jokes, the bawdiness, the put-downs, the self-deprecation, the silly names for our genitals, or the jibes at the opposite sex. Without shaming others or censoring ourselves. Without focusing on "performance" or "pleasing your partner." First, we need to unravel a lot of our sexual conditioning, though.

Let's Talk about "Shoulds," Maybe?

Ah, sexual conditioning. A system of beliefs that are intended to protect us from getting hurt but instead have kept us all so disconnected and scared of each other that we end up wounded anyway. You know the ones—the ones that got twisted somewhere and gave us words like "sluts," "players," "f★★k boys," "creeps."

This menagerie of myths can lead us into saying "yes" when we mean "no" and "no" when we want to say "yes." We say "yes" to the man who seems like good relationship material, who has the good job and the stable future, even though inside our body we feel nothing. We say "no" to the man who's uglier than us, who's a bit fatter and laughs too loudly, even though there's something about him that is so sexy. We shut down the impulse when we're attracted to someone of the same sex and pretend it's merely admiration, when our genitals know otherwise. We decide to settle down because we think we ought to or because we actually like someone.

The list of "rules" we've been taught about sex and relationships is long and wonderfully general. Here are a few you might have. Recognize any?

★ Men always want sex and/or only want sex.
★ Men use women for sex.
★ Women deny men sex to punish and control them.
★ If a romantic partner/date does something for me, I must reward them with sex.

★ Withholding sex is a good way to get into a relationship.

★ You shouldn't have to wait longer than a month of dating before you have sex with someone.

★ If you have sex with someone right away, they won't respect you.

★ We can only have sex if we want a relationship.

★ Only people who are objectively of the same attractiveness should have sex.

★ Women who have sex with you quickly are easy and sluts.

★ Men who want sex or pursue lots of partners are creeps.

★ Sex without penetration isn't sex.

★ Men need to ejaculate to have a good time.

★ You must know how to please your partner and always bring them to orgasm.

★ If I am not good in bed or always available, I am a bad partner.

None of these statements is true in any sense that's useful. Men do not always want sex; just like women, they get tired and stressed or don't feel sexy. The human need for affection and partnership isn't gendered. We've all "used" sex at one time or another—for physical relief, as distraction, for thrills, as a "reward," or to avoid actual intimacy. Doesn't make it right, or even particularly effective for what we're using it for, but it doesn't mean we do it all the time or that it's a specific gender problem. Just because a woman sleeps with you quickly doesn't mean she's sleeping with everyone quickly; also, why do you care? You don't own her. There's not a specific time frame by which you should have sex or not, in any relationship. No quotas. This is merely insecurity unloading itself as judgment. If you're only going to have sex with people you're in a relationship with, or going to be in a relationship with, you're either going to end up not having a lot of sex or end up being in relationships with people you don't really like. Similarly, men are not creeps just because they have a large sexual appetite and don't know how to express themselves well. That's a big ol' label you've stuck on them because you feel uncomfortable with their attention and saying no. Sex without penetration is still sex. Some of the most intense sexual experiences to be had are *sans* penetration. If you don't believe me, try it. Only 20 percent of women climax through vaginal penetration. Think outside the box. Expand your mind, and expand your pleasure. It's not all about climax, but about connection and intensity. Sex ends when one person has had enough. And "had enough" doesn't mean when they have orgasmed and it doesn't mean it's not been great; it's just, sometimes, the moment passes.

When we buy into these beliefs wholesale, we get our hearts and genitals all wrapped up, feeling fairy tales that aren't true. We block physical intimacy, heaping a whole load of meaning and stories on sex that are so far from the simple truth: two people enjoying intimate physical connection.

Sex means nothing more than the act itself. That's it. When you have sex, that is all you sign up for: a little opportunity for connection. I'm using words like "nothing more" and "that's all," but actually sex in this way is pretty special. It doesn't need an overlay of cultural conditioning—or fear and possessiveness—to try to make it something it isn't. I believe sex can be more sacred when we do it for its own sake, rather than wrapping it up in power dynamics and game playing, ultimatums and "must-haves." We don't need all the symbolism and covert significance—it's beautiful as it is.

It's hard to feel only this, though, about sex—there are always things that are going to creep in. Old fears that will pop up and need attending to, and little beliefs that are still present: that maybe he should stay the night if he respects you, for example. It's good to investigate and stay true to what yours are before you create any type of passionate connection, because often we aren't aware of them, or we assume everyone shares our beliefs, and then we get hurt when these uncommunicated personal conditions aren't honored.

There's a lot of talk about foreplay, but a lot of us forget to discuss after-sex before sex, which I think is just as important, if not more. How we like to be held, and how long we want body contact to continue in that afterglow. If we want them to stay over. If this means we are now "serious." What does honoring your connection look like to you? Do they check in with you in the following days to see how you are? Do you agree to meet again afterward? Are you now exclusive? To avoid feeling too vulnerable after sex, here are three questions to consider asking yourself before it:

1. Do you want to be intimate with this person right now?
2. Do you know what you need to feel safe: emotionally and physically—before, during, and after?
3. Can you communicate this and can you trust that it will be listened to?

Trust is a funny thing when it comes to sex. One of the reasons we can have such amazing experiences with each other during sex is because we are embodied humans, but it's the very same thing that makes us so fallible—and both ourselves and our partners unpredictable emotionally. The most we can ever do is learn how to trust in ourselves, know our own value, and trust that we will be able to cope with whatever curveballs are thrown; maybe our partner doesn't reply to our calls after sex, and we can learn from that experience—what happened there, and what we could do to help ourselves next time.

Good sex gets us out of our heads and overthinking everything, and into our bodies, where we "experience." When we do this, quite often those feelings are so strong and so pleasurable that they manage, indeed require us, to do the thing that we resist doing in all other areas of our life—surrender to the sensation and the moment. Utterly blissful and also pretty terrifying—it can feel disorientating and vulnerable to come back to Earth, and we can get all sorts of wires crossed.

Sometimes we get confused and mistake surrendering to the moment and the sensation in our bodies for surrendering ourselves to another human being. That can make partnerships needlessly strained—one person feels scared, as if they have handed themselves over and now need their partner to take full responsibility for them, and the other feels daunted by that challenge. Really all that's happened is that we've had an intensely pleasurable experience of letting go. It doesn't mean *not asking* for what you want to feel connected, whether that's cuddles or pillow talk, but it does mean not handing over total power for your welfare to your partner.

Another place we risk handing our power away is when we outsource responsibility for our sexual pleasure to our partner. Good sex requires *you* to know what you like and be able to ask for it. It also needs you to know what you don't like and how to communicate that. Your pleasure is your own responsibility. It is not up to your partner to know exactly how to please you. Of course, it might be preferable if your partner is willing to listen and get a little curious themselves—and maybe you could be willing to listen to them in return, mix their desires with yours, and get a little curious too—but it's not your or their obligation or job to know what either of you wants without communicating it. So often, either we don't know what we like or we won't ask for it. This means we'll just let them keep rubbing in the wrong places and label them bad in bed, all the while not giving them any chance to make it right. Maybe we tell ourselves, "This is just as good as sex gets for me."

There is a well-used myth: *that orgasms are given.* The truth is, no one "gave" you anything or "did" anything to you—those feelings are yours and you own them. They happened in your body—no one handed them to you, and no one can take them away. You show up ready to have an orgasm, and it naturally happens. It's not your fault if your partner is not getting off, and it sure as hell is not your trophy if they are. And vice versa.

And then there is the other way we don't take responsibility: when we outsource our emotional response to our partner. If they say "no" to sex, we think they're no good and they're in the wrong. The truth is, your feelings around this "no" are yours to take care of—your sensitivity to rejection. Maybe your partner just has a preference for no sex right now?

Experiment with making a list of what works for you, then divide that list into the following:

★ **Turn-on triggers:** things that turn you on straight away, even if you weren't thinking of sex already or aren't in the mood—this can include things people say, how they act, or what they do

★ **Pleasure menu:** things that turn you on during sex or physical connection—places you like to be touched and how you like them touched

★ **Turn-offs:** things that really slow you down or that have to be adjusted before you can be in the moment and enjoy sex

Putting this "list" into practice, if anything doesn't feel good during sex, slow down and gently talk; tell each other what floats your boat. If there are times when you are just not available sexually—tell them. This is particularly useful if you have a long-term partner—know when you just don't want sex so that you can tell them "There are times when, if you instigate sex with me, I am more likely to say 'no.'" It might be late on a "school night," maybe you have your period, or you just aren't in the mood. Stand by your feelings, and don't confuse "no" and "yes."

Knowing what your turn-off triggers are can be just as helpful as knowing what turns you on. Three that often strangle libido are expectation, worry, and lack of safety.

Expectation is a massive passion killer. For example, if I think I am being expected to do something—whether that's climax myself or make my partner climax—then it feels much less fun: like a task, rather than an experience. If that's you, then it's a good idea to set a time boundary—say, for example, that you touch for a half-hour, rather than aim for climax, which may or may not arrive. There's some logic here too—orgasms are a bit like sleep in that the more you try to force them, the less likely they are to come. Unwanted expectation can hang around the notion that physical intimacy has to include genitals or breasts. Stroking arms or kissing necks can be just as intimate. Embrace the feeling you have in your whole body more, rather than simply making love and paying attention to the "sexy" parts. The back of the knee, the ankles, and the inside of the wrist can also be potential and underappreciated erogenous zones. The one thing that corrupts sex the most is that we can't just experience touch for what it is. No one, while stroking a cat, suddenly turns around and tells the cat, "My turn. I've stroked you for twenty minutes now." It's just understood that stroking in and of itself is a pleasurable experience for both. However, in sex, we have a tendency to get very obligated and transactional—and only by breaking this mind-set can we see what we are doing.

Worry and lack of safety make sense as turnoffs. When a woman orgasms, the vigilance center in her brain—the part that keeps her safe—switches off. So a woman needs to be able to relax to climax. The thing is, your worries, your feeling unsafe, are not anybody's responsibility to provide, even your partner's. You can ask for things that help, though. These might be a commitment to hold you afterward, to go slow, or to reassure you that if you change your mind at any point, they will stop. (They should anyway, but it can often be comforting to communicate this again.)

Design Your Own Sex Life

I believe that humans can develop the emotional maturity, communication skills, and internal safety to have good sex outside of a committed, monogamous relationship without abandoning their higher selves. It's all about intention, responsibility, and willingness.

Your sexual connections can look however you want them to, but in my opinion it's preferable to have an intention that honors you both as adults indulging in pleasure together, rather than using each other for relief. Take casual sex seriously. Have an intention (like being in the moment) that honors you both. Say what you want and what you don't want. Be willing to listen, and be willing to f**k it up.

The journey to good sex involves a lot of less-than-good sex. That's okay. It doesn't mean anything other than this sex was not as pleasurable—it doesn't make the person a bad lover or person; it doesn't mean there's something wrong with you. At the end of the day it's all just sensation. If you can learn something from it, great! If not, then just relax and allow the next time to roll on by.

Community

There's an African proverb, "It takes a village to raise a child." Essentially, it means that one human needs an entire community of people to help grow into an adult (I think it also means it takes a village to support the mom and dad). But diaper rash and sleepless nights aside, this proverb also applies to anyone who wants to step into their full potential, to access the generous, loving, talented, calm, and creative human being that lives inside us all.

It might seem appealing, even glamorous, to forge ahead in the world solo: autonomous and wholly self-sufficient. Lord knows, I've thought of myself as a lone wolf more than once; lone wolves are known for being stronger, more aggressive, and more dangerous. The image of this solitary beast in the snow battling the odds for survival is seductive to anyone who has had to face challenges to get ahead—whether it's fixing the photocopier, struggling to pay the rent independently, or navigating a difficult emotional situation. If you're ambitious, talented and want to make a change, it can be surprisingly easy to get hypnotized by your own power and vow to do it on your own.

The thing about lone wolves in the wild, however, is that they can only hunt small prey or scavenge. To take down bigger animals, wolves need to hunt in packs. Very few lone wolves remain on their own indefinitely—almost all wolves join another pack, despite being rejected by their initial group.[21]

What we can learn from the lone wolf analogy is that it is not wise to hunt solo forever. Success is more likely to come for you through cooperation and shared aims. There is a great quote by Zig Ziglar: "You can have everything in life you want, if you will just help others get what they want."[22]

A pack of wolves is stronger because its strength relies on its component wolves—or "two heads are better than one"—so, just from nature, we can observe that the need to belong, to be part of a community, is a primal one. In my experience, the best way to value community, and its power, is to join or create one. It is the most nourishing way to expand into the person you are fully capable of being and achieve all the amazing things you can accomplish. This section is going to explore how to get the most out of the communities you're already a de facto member of (work, sports teams, family) as well as the ones you might discover and even, if you dare, create yourself.

I've been calling it a community. You could call it a tribe (that's trendy right now), a gang (though traditionally this has negative connotations), an "order" (also has a bit of baggage), a company, a team, a group, a collective (quite nineteenth century), a congregation, a sorority, a fraternity, a club, a cult (if you're starting a cult, make sure it's friendly and you may want to avoid talking about or serving Kool-Aid), a union, an association, or, if it gets really big … a movement. There are a lot of words for humans in groups, perhaps because we're deeply social creatures, naturally inclined toward cooperation. What I mean, loosely, when I reference community, is a group of people with something in common—a shared interest, shared values or needs, a shared location, a shared identity, or a shared cause. Emotional connections form between group members and everyone is (for better or worse) involved in some way—contributing and benefiting from the existence of the group as a whole.

Knowing that you can rely on and trust in a group shields you from the unnecessary worry that a lone wolf endures; if you don't know how to solve a problem, you can feel secure that there will always be people available for support—that even if you are not particularly close to them, they will help you in a time of need, not because they are choosing to be charitable, or because they will get something back from you, but because of your shared bond.

Communities provide individuals with the courage to take risks toward their goals, grabbing opportunities that they otherwise may have felt too insecure to take alone; with the sounding board and support of a community, that leap into the unknown seems less dangerous. Feeling the backing of a community, and knowing that, if you fail, there will be someone from your community waiting with a trampoline, ready to bounce you back up again, provides an incredible sense of freedom in and of itself, but community provides a lot more than that. It feeds one of our primal needs: that of belonging.

American psychologist Abraham Maslow proposed—in his 1943 paper "A Theory of Human Motivation"—a hierarchy of needs that all humans have.[23] It was arranged in a pyramid, with physiological needs at the bottom (food, water, rest, warmth). Safety needs next. And third, sandwiched in the middle of the pyramid, are belongingness and love needs.

Being part of a group provides a vital sense of belonging. When we are in a community, we experience acceptance—we are welcomed by others and feel valued as part of a group. It is vital to have a sense of our own intrinsic value separate from this, but being part of a community can also reflect our own worth back to us as we contribute to it, and help us on that journey toward finding ourselves, our worth, our strengths, and our unique gifts as individuals. This may quiet an anxious striving within us, a fear that drives us on—desperation to achieve simply because, if we don't, we aren't valuable. Being part of a community with a shared bond sends the message that we are worthy because we like and are liked by others—that we are enough. This leaves us free to achieve what we want to do, instead of pushing aggressively for accomplishment because our worth depends on it. Striving for acceptance from the community only devalues our sense of self, as opposed to the ideal situation, which is where outside approval complements our sense of intrinsic value and bolsters a positive self-image.

Above Belonging on Maslow's pyramid, come Esteem, Prestige, and Accomplishment, and, at the top, Self-Actualization—achieving one's full potential, including creative activities. Belonging might sit in the middle, but "community" can help provide *all* of the needs on the pyramid. Community security, leading to personal freedom, is the type of cooperation and sharing that provides you with a huge amount of knowledge, motivation, and meaning.

Knowing how you interact in a group is invaluable in teaching you how you communicate and what types of roles you gravitate toward playing—and those you avoid. They can give you a chance to practice leading—as well as what makes a good worker or supportive deputy. Whether you like to rebel or make yourself invisible. It's great to notice yourself doing these things and ask yourself why. Noticing these natural inclinations, and questioning *why* you feel them, can help you to uncover more about yourself: Are there potential roles you could be playing but haven't had the confidence to embrace yet? Playing just one role in a community restricts you and stops you from relating to others, as well as preventing you from suggesting improvements that benefit the community as a whole.

Listening is great, but if all you can do is listen, whatever inner analysis and problem-solving you may be doing will go unheeded and make no contribution to the collective.

Similarly, leading is a wonderful skill, but if you can only lead, you'll always be dependent on people being willing to follow. Being able to take on a whole kaleidoscope of roles, a talent we learn in community, gives you more freedom to act in a way that best suits any given situation we come across in life and allows you to empathize with others in similar roles. Don't hate the driver until you've been one, basically.

Just through being part of a number of large online conversations with multiple participants at any given time, I've noticed how I like to take part in community in a number of different ways: how I like to rush in to take care of people with a problem. Even if that means I feel uncomfortable about voicing opinions against those of the majority, or that I worry I'm talking too much or being ignored. Community is the glue that keeps us together when we want to disconnect or isolate ourselves—and those places are valuable for teaching us about ourselves and how we relate to others: how we can move through conflict instead of just abandoning ship when things become trying.

Growth

If you're doing community right, it will affect you right to your very bones. Although communities pull together because they have a shared cause, interest, or bond, not everyone, to use a phrase from a particularly snobbish politician I once interviewed, will always belong to the group of "people like us."

You are probably going to be thrown together with some difficult characters: bossy ones, ignorant ones, people who think toilet humor is funny when you don't, those you consider snooty and pretentious, highly offensive people who offend easily, sock-and-sandal wearers who think it's acceptable to comment on your fashion sense, etc., etc.

You may have consciously chosen this community (say by joining a sports/arts club, choir, women's institute, or fundraising committee) or unconsciously found yourself with them (moved to a new area, put on a team at work, family). Either way, they present you with a challenge.

Entering (or being thrown) into a new group of people is always the moment all your insecurities, the chips on your shoulder, and your worst social anxieties start vying for dominance of the floor. A dance troupe of your personal demons that otherwise no one gets to see. Contributing to a community can be tortuous on our egos, but it illuminates all our private self-deceptions. Yes, communities can, and very often do, bring out the worst in us. From those snide initial snap judgments we make about other members (hopefully in our heads), to posturing for dominance, or shrinking from visibility. All these behaviors are automated reactions based on our desire to establish a foothold, find our role in the group, and feel secure, validated, and useful. As awful as these struggles sound, this is actually good news, because once you can see and feel these behaviors at work, you can change them for something more constructive.

I've been a member of a number of different communities in my time, from meditation groups to roommates to work projects (and let's not forget extended family Christmases). Every time, I swagger in with some idea that I'm a fully actualized, emotionally mature, spiritually aligned adult with excellent communication skills. Every time, I'm stomach-churningly humbled to discover I have more to learn. When I'm working as part of a group, my insecurities resurface— I sometimes find myself holding back and not contributing because, though I could help, I'm afraid what I have to offer won't be good enough and I'll be embarrassed.

Then there's another side of me that emerges—my superiority complex, which is challenged by the community itself. I might find myself thinking, "I'm so much better than this person. I don't need them." Other times my patience is stretched ("Lord, it would be so much quicker if I just did it myself"). Then there are those fears of scarcity—that there isn't enough, I won't get enough, and I don't have enough— although if I'm honest, those appear every time my table orders a dish to share at a restaurant (my friend takes all the best parts while I'm in the bathroom).

Contribute, Cooperate, Create

One of the reasons communities are challenging is because they require you to contribute—quite often in front of a group of people. Although you may have a shared bond with these people, you largely don't know them well. You might be asked to introduce yourself and tell people a little about yourself and what you can contribute to the group. This can make you feel intensely vulnerable. At first, you do it based on trust alone, and, although you get much out of community, according to how open and active you are willing to be, these benefits aren't always obvious overnight.

Personally, all of the above challenges my natural "lurker"—the side of me that likes to sit on the sidelines and watch, rather than take part. If you have lurker tendencies, too, you're not alone—the 1 percent rule in internet culture is the general observation that in online communities only 1 percent create the content and the other 99 percent simply lurk. The "90–9–1" version of this rule states that for websites where users can both create and edit content, 1 percent of people create content, 9 percent edit or modify that content, and 90 percent view the content without contributing. The openness required to be in community can be immensely challenging—but it also allows you to realize parts of yourself: both your generosity and your inner miser.

The openness required by community has been a great teacher for me. I refer to everything that is hideously uncomfortable and that I don't enjoy as "a great teacher." Try it—it's fun. Semantic tricks like this appeal to my dark sense of humor; e.g., "That boyfriend was a great teacher for me" (he cheated on me twice).

I like to think that, if I at least learn from the teacher the first time, the same lesson isn't going to come back around again. Cultivating an attitude of openness is a hard lesson but has taught me to embrace and appreciate others' perspectives.

Collectively, this allows us to create richer narratives, more welcoming dialogues, and more meaningful conversations, better projects, and better outcomes. Essentially, by increasing your willingness to share what you have others are generally more likely to share more of what they have with you. In so doing, your community pools its resources, be they material, intellectual, creative (even emotional or spiritual in the context of support or prayer groups) to achieve its shared aims.

The growing industry of crowdfunding is a perfect example of how communities converge to harness the power of collective resources—where individuals are inspired to donate what they can to a project, brand, event, relief effort, or campaign after reading about it online. Some fundraising targets can be exceeded many times over, and the joy of being able to achieve your goals from a platform built by people who may not know you at all, but care enough to share their hard-earned money with you, can be truly heartwarming. It also serves as a reminder of our intrinsic goodness, and how good it feels to give, restoring our faith in humanity when we see people who reach into their pockets to give what they can.

When you're taking part in community it's really easy to look around the table (town hall, gazebo, video conference call, or whatever meeting venue is used by your particular group) when something is being discussed and think, "I don't want to share this here; these people don't deserve my knowledge/ideas/skills/time." You might think, "I can't be bothered ... this isn't my responsibility," even though you have a shared interest with these people and a vested interest in this community succeeding. Perhaps one member of the community is being particularly vocal and irritating you—so you sit, silent and smug, safe in the knowledge you have more experience in that area and are better placed to serve up a solution. You might not want to offer your help because you see it as the group feeding off you, or you might even worry that someone may steal your ideas and claim the credit. This sort of jealous protection is bonkers, irrational, and limiting. It is, however, very common, and motivated rarely by reality, but by our own fears—a toxic cocktail of inferiority with a shot of bitterness and a little superiority cherry on top. Delicious.

There are a few different ways to handle this feeling—the approach I've found most rewarding, however, is to stop conceiving of myself as "sharing" my resources and instead plug into the idea that I'm contributing to creating something bigger. It has the effect of making me feel much more generous, focused, and bound to a higher creative purpose.

It's Not about "Working for Free"

There's respecting your value and honoring your talents or the business you have built, and then there's jealously guarding an accumulated stash of skills, ideas, and knowledge until it actually ends up impeding your growth.

Those who get grabby like this remind me of Smaug, the dragon from *The Hobbit*. Dragons famously sleep on piles of gold and attack anyone who comes close. There's mixed consensus on this, but one reason dragons do so is apparently because of their one weakness: They set everything on fire! So they can't sleep on normal bedding. Another possible reason suggested for dragons sleeping on piles of gold is that the gold embeds itself into the dragon's soft underbelly and forms an armor. We are not dragons. We are naturally cooperative creatures. We do not have the dragon's weakness. We don't need to be terrifying fire-breathing monsters guarding our gleaming hoard.

A life lived on the defensive is no life at all. It means you can't relax. Hence why dragons sleep with one eye open. If you adopt Smaug's attitude, you'll only feel peaceful when you have nothing left to protect.

I'm no monk; I don't believe having no possessions is the route to freedom or happiness. I think it's possible to be openhearted and generous, while asking to be paid what I feel I deserve, when relevant. Community is a great place to find out where this fine line is drawn—and guess what! The lines can shift under your feet before you know it.

Teamwork Makes the Dream Work

I went on a spirituality retreat once, and like so many of these weekends, it was astronomically expensive. As with all of these experiences, it began with the deeply sacred practice of paying vast amounts of money to be made to feel immensely uncomfortable.

I'm exaggerating. There was electricity and hot water, and we were actually cooked for. However, after our first meal in our new rudimentary accommodation, one of the course leaders stood up and started dividing the cleaning duties between us for the weekend. I'll tell you what: The ferocity of my expression and the fire in my chest meant I felt pretty Smaug-esque at that point. I had *not* paid an extortionate fee to clean toilets and scrub dishes.

> Altruistic behavior happens in the animal world too. For example, humpback whales are known to rescue seals from killer whales, swimming in, dispersing the pod of killers, and allowing the seal to escape.

However, there was something wonderful about the whole experience that I'm not sure I could have gained another way. The first thing was that I had to work with people to get the job done as quickly as possible, which meant I had to get on with them, and appreciate their value in helping me work. The second is that it was wonderfully leveling. I was giving my time and energy away for free, but I felt more part of the experience, more connected with everyone there, more part of the whole setup where we stayed. I felt valuable and somehow lighter: less weighed down by my own self-importance. It felt like, working together, we had created something special.

In Sikhism, they call this *seva*—or selfless service—and it's a way of getting closer to God. Sikhs are taught that inner peace and freedom comes from *seva*, a serenity that cannot be found elsewhere. Kamalpreet Badasha, a British writer in her thirties who lives in London and was raised as a Sikh, spent Sundays at the gurdwara with her grandmother performing *seva*: "As a child I would help make *roti* (flatbread), serve food, and wash dishes for the free communal kitchen. Only as I grew older did I realize how unique this routine was from a world perspective. . . . *Seva* for me is a way of getting closer to that pure energy of doing something for the greater good."

Sharing Can Mean Growth—For You and for the Community

The word "sharing" means divide up, but I don't think that's the case when we share things like our time, ideas, or skills in community.

Some might say it's more like "giving them away," but that's not quite true either. Information and insight are not pizza— you don't have fewer slices if you offer some up. What are you really giving away? No one can take your knowledge from you. Sharing your passions, thoughts, or talents only reaffirms them, refines them, and energizes them. Sharing in this way is a creative force—it strengthens and deepens these abilities and gifts. Were they really yours to cling onto anyway? Most of the time we learn from or are inspired by other people. We should embrace sharing our skills, knowledge, or ideas. If we should be wary of anything at all, it is not using them— or not applying them well. Unused tools get rusty; it is the same with the brilliance inside of us.

However, we get all protective and competitive and withdraw. Half the time we're so focused on thinking we have everything to lose that we can't see all there is to gain. We forget that, in a community, whatever we contribute to the pot is returned to us threefold, in ways we can't imagine yet. None of us can predict the future. We can never know how much we may depend on others in the years to come.

The ancient fable of "The Lion and the Mouse" by Aesop is a perfect illustration of how our actions in the present can come back to us later in life. In the story, the lion is about to kill a mouse who has disturbed his slumber. When the mouse begs for forgiveness, the lion shows mercy and lets the mouse go. When the lion is later captured by hunters, the mouse recalls his leniency and gnaws through the ropes, freeing the lion.[24]

What the fable teaches us is that when we're the ones with the skills, we feel powerful and in demand, but there may be a time when these skills are useless in the face of an unforeseen need and we turn to someone else in the community for help. This has happened to me time and time again. Sometimes, the person I least expected to help me is the one who offers a kind smile and says something that totally throws my life into perspective on a rough day. The person I hated on my first day at work becomes my best friend.

We need each other in ways we fail to recognize. The biggest lie we tell ourselves is that we are self-sufficient. One of my friends who recently started taking antidepressants told me she was embarrassed to rely on them. "Where's the shame in that?" I asked her. I started to list all the things we rely on: We don't know how to fix our own toilet, so we call a plumber. We rely on the city to take away our garbage. Most of us don't know how recycling is sorted. We rely on food companies that supply supermarkets. We rely on so many things from so many people—and most of the time we don't even acknowledge it until something goes wrong. We are social animals that have dominated this planet (perhaps too effectively) because of our ability to cooperate. Self-sufficiency for its own sake is simply insecurity driving us backward. We create best in collaboration. Things grow when we come together.

That's why one question I am guided by when at a crossroads is: "What am I making this decision based on?" Choosing not to help the community may be a decision based on *fear*—fearing that I won't get any benefits or that I will experience negative effects from it.

A decision based on fear is never fruitful. It restricts rather than encourages growth. The course and nature of every living thing is determined by growth. Every living thing on this planet—from plants to animals to humans—is designed to grow, to thrive, to *become*. Growth is the fuel for the purpose of, and the timekeeper for, life's journey. As William S. Burroughs writes in *Junky*: "When you stop growing you start dying."[25]

If you remove fear from the decision-making process, you begin to make choices that broaden your outlook, expanding your realm of possibility. Deciding how best to act in ways that promote growth means you fall into harmony with life. You become more open, and then, inspiring yourself and others, you begin creating. When we share knowledge or skills, we are generating more; we strengthen relationships, gain fresh perspectives, and refine and cultivate our insights. Offering these gifts up to a community you are part of generates more energy, adding to the resource pool that you and your skills are also part of. This collaborative spirit allows us to cooperate, to create something bigger than oneself. It's an immensely freeing experience, to relinquish ego for a time and give yourself up to the service of a shared aim, especially on those days when we self-importantly feel everyone depends on us.

Communities are a meaningful anchor when we get carried away on a storm cloud of anxiety about our own lives, reminding us that we are not the center of the world. It's good to be a member of different communities for this reason, to dip in and out and know that there are worlds within worlds. They can give us perspective: There is more to life than just us—and actually that's a good thing. It helps us see ourselves clearer—as whole individuals, but also as part of many "wholes." Think of yourself as a part of a ginormous Venn diagram, rather than a lonely circle looking in.

The Games We Play

This idea is expressed in James P. Carse's book *Finite and Infinite Games*.[26] He writes: "No one can play a game alone. One cannot be human by oneself. There is no selfhood where there is no community. We do not relate to others as the persons we are; we are who we are in relating to others."

Carse's theory is that we play (at least) two kinds of games in this world: finite ones, where the purpose is to win, and infinite ones, where the goal is to keep the game going.

Carse's book inspired me to question my motives in a different way in order to help me choose the best course of action when I'm tempted to withdraw or become begrudging. I ask myself: *Does this decision allow everyone to win, or just me?* or *How can I play here so everyone gets to keep playing?*

Experience the Placebo Effect but with People

Being part of a community requires you to contribute to the growth of the group by making available your skills, ideas, time, or knowledge to enrich the spiritual and physical wealth of the whole, of which you, too, are a part. You open at least some of yourself and your resources to create something greater than yourself, essentially based on trust. It's not possible to know for sure if your contribution will be appreciated; ideally, the most nourishing communities will cultivate an environment where such generosity is valued, though.

Similarly, you can't know if your offering will be abused or if you yourself will benefit because of this faith. My experience in my varied roles as a coach, a journalist, a social media producer, an employee, and a manager is that if you treat people as if they were kind, capable, even powerful human beings, they usually surpass your expectations.

Assume people are assholes, and they usually won't disappoint. Though, guess what? Assuming people are assholes is also kind of an asshole thing to do. When you pause to examine your motives, asking yourself questions like *Is fearful thinking prompting me to make this decision?* and *Am I playing for everyone to keep playing or just for one person, myself, to win?*—and choose instead the courageous, confident decision that allows everyone to win—your actions are affirming a positive view of humankind, of which you are one. Aside from the fact you get to experience your own exalted humanity, you are also believing the best of others, which more often than not results in others doing the same for you. It's a phenomenon I like to call practicing the placebo effect with people.

Practicing the placebo effect with people means expecting them to be brilliant. It means acting based on trust that they will mostly choose to do the best thing, the thing that uplifts rather than denigrates community ties, without a bit of doubt in their goodness. Of course, sometimes we will be disappointed. I like Abraham Lincoln's words on this: "If you trust, you will be disappointed occasionally, but if you mistrust, you will be miserable all the time." True, he did get shot in a theater, so you could argue that trust didn't help him in the end, but then again he also is consistently voted one of the best presidents of the United States ever, who preserved the Union and set the wheels in motion to abolish slavery. At the end of the day, do you want to live a big life or a small life? If you want to reach your full potential, you need to care about community, which means giving a f**k about creating, and that requires you to trust, and invest, in other humans.

The problem with building walls around our resources is that walls work both ways. We become so restricted and closed off that we also block the possibility of freely receiving. We're so busy making sure no one shortchanges us that we can't see the gifts people are willing to hand us, gratis.

Some Questions to Ask Yourself about Growth in a Community Context

1. First, take a moment to consider your role in a particular community you are part of. What role do you play now? Is this role the one you want? Is it best suited to your talents?
2. Now consider your community, its aims, and its purpose: How do you want your community to grow?
3. What can you provide to contribute to this growth?

Other Things to Consider

4. To see the growth you want for the community, will your role need to change? If so, how? What inspiration can you take from other members in creating a shared vision for the future?

Work

In a village, far away, nestled on the hillside of the semireality where all fables, allegories, and parables take place, there lived a man who was always cold. Standing out looking at the stars one night, naked and shivering, he finally decided he needed to take action about his temperature. Why not make a coat? He spotted some wild sheep in the distance and went out to catch them.

At first he struggled, so he got a lasso. He was warmed up by the exercise but was still feeling cold. So he lassoed some more. He got so busy in this activity that sometimes he forgot he was cold. Nonetheless, he was determined, and every night he went out, rounding up more and more sheep. Soon he had a whole flock. His body ached occasionally, and most of the time he remained cold, only now he was frustrated. He thought to himself, "The sheep were meant to make me warm. Maybe I just need more sheep." He spent his whole life herding until finally he realized what the problem was. He'd forgotten to make a coat.

This is what a lot of us do in our careers. We spend all our time accumulating money and power, getting bigger salaries and more responsibilities, but money and power are never what we really want. They are just ways we think we can get what we want. And we're so busy getting them, we totally lose touch with why we wanted them in the first place.

We go to work to make money; it's true. We need to feed and house and dress ourselves. But if money is your main reason for going to work, then you're shortchanging yourself, either by what you're doing or by the way you're doing it.

We spend a third of our adult lives at work. We owe it to ourselves to make sure the work we do gives us more than bigger bank balances. If all your job amounts to is you exchanging your time for money, I promise you, you're getting a bad deal. I think we need three things to make our work work for us, aside from being able to pay the bills, and that is having a job that adds value, that allows us to learn something (or progress), and that gives us some sort of enjoyment.

How Do I Help?

You don't have to be a rocket scientist, brain surgeon, or all-star athlete to see value in your work. It's about how you relate to the work you do.

If you're a supermarket cashier who talks with customers in a way that brightens their day, then you may find your value there. If you see your role as a cleaner as being about transforming environments into nice places to live and work, so that people feel better once you've been in a space, then this might increase your sense of value too. We all want to be appreciated at work, but we must first seek to find and appreciate this intrinsic value for ourselves, or our self-esteem ends up being at the mercy of our boss's capacity for compliments. This appreciation of our job's value must be felt viscerally. It's not something that can be dictated to you, but a personal discovery.

There's a story in Andro Donovan's excellent book *Motivate Yourself.*[27] Three men are hard at work with shovels, digging. A woman walks by, stops by the first one, and asks him: "What are you doing?"

"I'm digging a hole, stupid," he replies.

The passerby walks up to the next worker and asks the same question. "What are you doing?" she asks.

"I'm constructing a wall," the second digger tells the woman.

And so she walks up to the third digger.

"What are you doing?" she asks.

"I'm building a cathedral," he replies.

Paid to Learn

Approaching the sticky, tough parts of your job with a view that they are essentially free training is one way to ease a little tightness around the challenges we all face at work. The places where your job is driving you crazy might be the spot where you are building up the most skills. Find it hard dealing with a difficult boss? You're learning how to manage up. Have a lot of different requests coming in all the time? You're learning how to prioritize, focus your attention, and say "no."

The goal is not so much to be good at your job, but to constantly have a job that allows you to get better. If you're 100 percent easy-breezy cruise-control good at your job, then your work isn't working for you. Mistakes are progress. If you're not failing frequently, then you're not playing big enough.

Enjoyment

The easiest way to make things fun is by doing them with others. If you can make friends at work, your life improves immensely. However, most of us have a natural reticence toward this, preferring to keep our distance or play politics to get ahead. We might be defensive or distrusting or hold back to avoid drama.

In my experience, when you have lots of humans working together, you get drama regardless. Trying to avoid it might be admirable, but I've always preferred to assume it's coming no matter what, so I might as well build friendships to make the drama worth it. Connections at work can be hard, however, especially if other employees want to keep to themselves, or you just don't naturally see eye to eye on things. But it's not about learning how to work with people you don't like; it's about learning how to like the people you work with. Make it a challenge—see if you can be the sort of person to bring out the best in others. Find a similarity, something you both share (and don't make it something negative—like you both hate your jobs or the boss). Chat about nonwork things—make it clear you are more than just a drone—and keep searching for something you both can connect on. Bring in food, share it, say hello and goodbye, and always offer to get coffee. Don't sit with your headphones on all day; invite people to go for a walk at lunchtime. Recognize people's talents, no matter how small. Be generous with your knowledge and time. There's always an opening for connection, even if it's the day the printer breaks. Be ready.

When It's Still Garbage

That said, there are always parts of our job we enjoy less. Maybe it's the admin, the form-filling, or the email management. It is boring and perfunctory and teaches us nothing, despite requiring our concentration. I've found a 90/10 rule works for me. As long as 90 percent of my job is doing the things I enjoy, where I'm learning, creating, and adding value, then I will put up with the other 10 percent. When it creeps over that line, I start to feel resentful, and the rest of my work suffers too.

What if what you enjoy is at a much lower percentage? Well, you can reframe it—looking for the value or challenge there. You can find a way to make it fun, or you can ask for it to be changed.

Sometimes, no amount of emotional levity can make the parts of your job you don't like easier, and you may want to ask management if you can change something. When something or someone is giving you grief at work, it can feel like an albatross hanging around your neck—especially if you've been struggling with it for some time and can't see how to make things better. The good news is, if you've tried to change something once and it didn't work, that doesn't mean the change will never happen. It simply means the way you tried to change it last time didn't work. So now you have more "data"—and next time, you'll want to try a different way and see if that works. The problem is not you and it's not what you want; it's just that the way you're trying to get it isn't effective. So many people find themselves facing an obstacle at work and make one or two similar attempts to surmount it and then, when they can't, assume it's impossible. It's madness. I think of them facing a door that has to be pulled open and repeatedly pushing it and then, when that fails, trying to use force to break it down and then, when that doesn't work, claiming the door is broken, or it's impossible to get through, or that they don't have the skills to open it. They do; it's just that they haven't worked out yet that they need to pull it to get to the other side. Try something different. Patience and creativity are your allies; use them.

Culture Clash

Sometimes communities promote certain values that clash with our own. It might be company principles you disagree with, or perhaps you feel at odds with the whole industry.

You might feel disappointed when you discover this conflict and feel that you should immediately leave. You might feel pressured into compliance. Hang tight. Healthy communities can thrive on dissent—it's actually not a matter of right or wrong (though you may feel it is)—and such conflict can be great for knowledge, growth, and creativity, both for the community and for yourself.

First things first: Don't get on your moral high horse. Values are immensely personal; they vary even within families. Even our own values change over time and in different contexts. It's why people say things like: "You get more right/left-wing as you get older." Or, perhaps, you might lose your enthusiasm for clubbing or hot pants.

Values are a bit like principles in that they are great for providing a strong backbone and can keep us motivated when we're tempted to go off the rails, but without some flexibility, they can become constrictive. Watch those who say "I am intensely principled" without further qualification. In reality, what they almost certainly mean is: "Do not disagree with me; I am incredibly rigid."

Cooperation in community requires flexibility—it doesn't necessarily mean compromising your authenticity, but it may mean putting yourself in someone else's shoes, so you can find out what and why the other person is thinking or acting as they are. Think inquisitively rather than defensively. Understanding before advancement.

Value clashes can be incredibly fruitful if approached correctly and can lead to beneficial culture change. But even if they don't, they are useful personally. First, acknowledge you've got a strong enough sense of yourself to distinguish between yourself and the collective, which is positive. It's very easy to lose a sense of selfhood in community or abandon yourself while attempting to be part of something bigger, so experiencing this clash is actually a healthy sign. Plus, sometimes we can come to use that sensation of conflict or dislike that arises inside of us when a value is expressed that we don't like (say, someone cheats or tells a white lie to get ahead and make a sale), to show us what we do like—that we really value honesty or fairness, for example. When your personal values come up against the collective, it's a great opportunity for growth, primarily because you will need to take some form of action—while doing so will be uncomfortable, not doing so or just going along with it is likely to feel extremely stressful too.

How to Approach a Culture Clash

This is where you need to get curious. See if you can find out why the person/organization you're clashing with thinks the way they do. This is about gathering information so you can understand and put your best case forward. Why does your boss want you to be available on email after work? Maybe she values devotion to the job? Is this her value, or is it company policy? If you can persuade her that setting tight boundaries between work and home allows you to be more present and effective at work when you're there, that this is actually a sign of your commitment and that the quality of attention you can give is more valuable when it's fully engaged, then you have a greater chance of being understood and being able to switch off after hours, without having to change workplaces.

Additionally, perhaps, there might be something for you to learn.

> There are many strange jobs in the world, and one of them is definitely a "snake milker." These people extract snake venom from poisonous snakes like cobras and sell it to hospitals or laboratories for antivenom. They are often employed by zoos or serpentariums and can make up to $2,500 a month.

When I was working for the BBC, I was initially incredibly frustrated by the bureaucracy and the huge number of approvals from manager upon manager that needed to be sought in order to get something done. There was a level at which it was not useful. However, there were also times when it was. My value of being creative first and foremost was clashing with their values of accuracy and reputation. Many frustrated conversations and one big mistake later, I realized those rules were there in order to protect me. The BBC was held in such high regard, was so trusted, that any errors were seen as sacrilegious by both audiences and other media organizations alike. Getting it wrong wasn't worth the short-term creative gain. They were risk-averse for a reason.

You can also find common ground. If you're working for a company, it's likely there are some things you have in common, so that is the first place to start—where your interests overlap. You might disagree on the how, but you both are aligned with the what (the success of the company, a good working environment), so that is something worth acknowledging as a base.

Finding out what they value, seeing how what you want fits, and using their language to spell that out helps. For example, the BBC has a number of core values, including creativity and trust, as well as to inform, educate, and entertain. If I show how risk is necessary as part of being creative, then it is likely managers will be more willing to listen to my "out there" ideas. Because I know they value their reputation, I might tap into that value to show how my creative (but risky) ideas could increase trust with audiences. Perhaps I frame the change I want to bring in in an audience-centric way. For example, to experiment with social media to reach more license-fee payers in a way that is natural to them. I focus on what they will gain from taking risks, and how these things are in line with their values.

It's important to frame your argument as visionary rather than in negative terms. I've never had success asking for something by talking about bad things. People want to be heroes, not accused of being bad managers. For example, saying I want an extra member of staff because the tasks we are meant to perform are failing without one would go down like a lead balloon. I have been much more effective getting management on my side when I have explained the positive effects of giving me a certain thing. In my experience, people prefer being associated with a successful outcome than with preventing or stopping a negative one. Go to a manager with a situation where you suggest things are already failing and they clam up immediately, because it's seen as an attack. However, if you explain how a project manager will bring in incredible results, setting an example to the rest of the company about the best way to run a department, then you make the prospect of hiring one seem much more exciting. We'd all rather be seen as the architect of some great success, rather than someone sweeping up dirt.

Of course, there may be times when the gap between company culture and your personal values is insurmountable. When that happens, it's time to leave, with as little resentment as possible. Leaving a community is always hard—but know that communities are made up of individuals and quitting a job doesn't mean you have to dissolve all the personal ties you've made. They are independent of the whole. While community—and the identity we find within it—can provide us with meaning and value, it is not the only way we are worthy. Losing or leaving your job does not mean a loss of identity, though it can feel that way. No one can take away your skills or what you learned in that role, even if the job itself is no longer part of your life.

Knowing when to quit is as valuable as knowing when to stay. Holding on to something that makes us miserable isn't a good message to send to our souls, no matter how much time or effort we've previously invested in making it work. Quitting something that doesn't serve us is simply making space for something better. Where you work and what you work as has to work for you, too, or you're selling yourself short.

Get in Touch with What Works for You at Work, or Not, by Asking Yourself These Questions

1. How does my job contribute to making other people's lives better/easier/more fulfilling?
2. How could I make it so that it does?
3. What would the impact be if I don't do my job well?

4. What do I find hard in this job?
   (This is what this job is teaching you.)
5. What do I know I am learning here?
6. What do I enjoy in my job?
7. What would be some ways to enjoy my job more?
8. Who would I like to connect with at work?
9. What percentage of things do I dislike doing or find pointless?

You should see a picture emerging. A clearer vision of your direction. Remember, all we need to do is take the next right step and trust that the one after that will reveal itself.

Social Media

Undoubtedly, social media has changed our communities, broadening them, deepening bonds, making it easier than ever to connect with others. We can now make "friends" with someone on the other side of the world, separated by thousands of miles, our respective cultures, our lifestyles, and our choices. We can (and do) fall in love through social media, and, just as fast as they can be made, friendships and connections can be broken. It is one of the fastest, cheapest, and most accessible ways to learn how to communicate well … and how to communicate badly.

How many times have you seen someone mortally offended in the comments section for an innocent-sounding joke? Social media reigns supreme in showcasing the full range of misunderstanding that our interactions are open to, the complexities of language, and what deeply emotional creatures we are. It offers magnificent examples of the human propensity to judge and blame, puffed up with self-righteousness, and of how awful we feel when the same behavior finds us on the receiving end.

Oh, yes, it's a fantastic tool for revealing (and thus healing) your insecurities. Seeing other people's beach vacation or wedding photos that suddenly make you feel a little wobbly in the tummy (or relationship department). It's hard to remedy flaws we can't detect, so actually noticing our fears here can be helpful, even if it does make us want to take up residence under a rock. Notice if you're jealous—and use that jealousy to acknowledge that whatever your friend's photo shows you might be something that you want. Remember, everything is edited.

> The first social media platform was sixdegrees.com, founded in 1999, when you still had to scan your pictures to upload them to your profile.

There's value in not editing yourself, though—in posting pictures of yourself that might make you feel self-conscious but once out there feel empowering. We can use social media to challenge ourselves in this way.

It's a good thing that our viewpoints on societal or political issues are also challenged online—despite talk of echo chambers, social media actually gives you access to a huge variety of different, as well as similar, views. In revealing our best and worst sides, the amount of information we can gain about ourselves by watching the way we choose to behave online is absolutely invaluable; what we hide and share alike.

Facebook, Twitter, Instagram, and YouTube, to name the big four, provide an unparalleled resource for studying the way humans interact. The rapidity and ease of forging connections on social media mean they are also a really powerful way to influence and leverage community.

This is why social media is important. You probably didn't log on to Facebook this morning thinking, "Right, I've got my coffee; now I want a simple, rapid way of powerfully leveraging community." But you probably will use it to talk to your friends, to see their news, and hear opinions, to share your news and to entertain yourself while you are on the train or waiting for a latte, idly scanning articles or scrolling through pictures.

If you want to get the most out of social media (and hey, with all your data it's certainly getting the most out of you) it's time to look at it through fresh eyes, for a purpose other than entertainment and keeping up with friends. Online communities can teach you about people—how truly social we are—and how to stay connected without being swallowed completely by them.

Thumbs Up or Thumbs Down?

"No man is an island," wrote John Donne in 1624. If, nearly 400 years ago, he recognized that as humans we were all fundamentally connected, then how much more resonant are his words now? Facebook is the second-most visited website in the world. A quarter of the world's population uses it every month. It is a serious tool that enables mass communication globally. Humans are social, and one characteristic of that, as discussed, is that we build community.

> The words "communication" and "community" come from the same root in Latin—"communis": common or shared.

Social media sites are a little like online Roman forums— these apps are marketplaces, coffee shops, newsstands, campaign grounds, information hubs, meeting places, and, of course, dating sites. According to Facebook, there are almost 5 billion pieces of content shared on the site every single day. With infinite chatter, stories, pictures, and ads all vying for our attention, what we then see is everyone trying to shout the loudest—and the communication at times is as savage and brutal as a gladiatorial arena.

When you log on, what you check into is your own little select community, created partly by whom you've chosen to follow or connect with, and partly curated by algorithms, which, more often than not, prioritize the most engaging, popular posts.

Then, within that, there are groups of dedicated communities—for fans, those with certain medical conditions, dog lovers, craftspeople, people who enjoy a certain sense of humor. You name it, and it's there. There are hashtags to follow on Twitter or Instagram, rules of engagement in some Facebook groups, and, on Reddit, there's a vast and complicated etiquette—in-jokes and admins weighing in to defuse conflict or even ban inappropriate users.

If online is community, then "posts" are what we use to build relationships and become a valued member of the group. This may sound obvious, but there's something about voicing opinions from behind a keyboard that makes us forget that this is really just all communication between people in a community. Online we seem to forget how communication actually works, and become emotional parodies or performances of ourselves. Perhaps all that this shows is how difficult communication is in the first place.

Popularity Versus Communication and Remembering to Be Human

Aside from the pressure social media induces to perform "in public," it's also used to "self-define." We are encouraged to self-define from the moment we first create a profile—a "bio"—to tell people about who we are.

When we share, we are associating ourselves with pieces of content. Our accounts are public scrapbooks of pictures, posts, and articles that we want to share with our communities—we value them and want others to value them (and by extension, us). We are really saying to our feed, "look at this (me)." Whatever the type of content, sharing it links it with our public image. It's why crime articles might be read a lot on online websites, but they aren't shared a lot. If you suddenly only shared grisly murder stories, wouldn't your friends be concerned? Generally, people just don't post such things, although we all read them, unless we're railing against this kind of violence or highlighting a misleading headline.

People largely share what they are very much for or what they are very much against. There's not much room for nuance.

One reason for this is the way we "consume" on social media—we are usually reading on small screens on cell phones, and simply skimming. We don't have the same emotional investment we might have when reading a book. Time and attention are the stocks and shares of a very big online economy, and a lot of people are competing for that real estate. There's no time for foreplay on social media. It's all quick climax. Long, complex posts require more brainpower and, frankly, that cute dog video is just more appealing.

Essentially, we want to tell people about ourselves, in a concise, punchy, clever way, that makes us look good and that people will read. We crave impact, more "followers," readership, a fan base. Impact is not nuance. We know the sort of posts that elicit strong responses in us and we want ours to elicit the same responses in others. We start to post only things we believe will be popular or engage our audience. If we aren't rewarded by that little dopamine hit from a notification alerting us we've captured a little (fleeting) attention, what's the point?

Social media is great for bringing out our inner egotist. We want to look good, and we want popularity. However, being popular on social media doesn't mean being liked— mostly, it means attention-grabbing, engaging, whatever prompts the greatest response. Certain types of emotion are more likely to entice people to "like" and share.

Jonah Berger, who authored a study published in the journal *Psychological Science*, found that posts that prompted a certain emotion were shared more. The aroused emotions— emotions that give us energy—like anger, fear, or humor, are more likely to drive people to share information: "If something makes you angry as opposed to sad, for example, you're more likely to share it with your family and friends because you're fired up."[28]

Social media power is engaged in popularity; to be popular, all you need to do is convince people to interact with you. Unfortunately, agents of chaos, provocateurs, and trolls can use this little secret to great effect. We all fall for the sensationalist/divisive posts that were designed to irritate us, to outrage us, baiting us to respond and ensure the post goes viral. It's a game, replete with psychological power plays, ethical posturing, heavy provocation, and a lot of copy-and-paste. We want fame and status. If we go viral enough, maybe we could become president and ruler of the free world too?

However, this doesn't work for everyone—as online audiences become more sophisticated, so does the type of communication that holds their attention. I've learned "tricks" in my time as a social media editor and producer for the BBC and the *Independent*, but, ultimately, valuing "celebrity" over a strong community of collaborators, sounding boards, and diverse viewpoints isn't a great plan. Like breakfasting on chocolate cake, it feels rich and exciting initially, but not so great when you crash soon after, nauseous from binging on garbage.

People may think they want vast armies of followers, but lots of followers don't guarantee "engaged" audiences—trust me, I've been on the back end, watching the numbers: celebrities with millions of followers, few of whom care enough to actually read or act on the celebrity's post. Such "stars" just don't have a strong enough relationship with the people in their community to really engage with them.

Conversely, there are people with a relatively small following who harness all of it and get their stories read and shared widely. Ask yourself the question—do you want people to simply recognize you, or do you want friends?

Because of the huge audiences available on social media, the strange hierarchy of verification and follower count (as well as the way individuals with large fan bases are fetishized), it's easy to get seduced by the fame and status that social media can offer any one of us. Social media allows anyone to be "special" once they've learned how to "hack" the platform—then we can bask in the illusory social power that comes with lots of followers/viewers and the constant notifications. I know one individual who simply shares a lot of missing people pictures on Twitter because it gets him retweets—and even when he knows the people have been found, he doesn't take the picture down. But, what (I'm dying to ask) is the point? You have thousands of followers—but for what?

There's a great story in Jainism that is related in a number of books by Osho. I read it in *Fear: Understanding and Accepting the Insecurities of Life*.[29] The tale is of a chakravartin—an all-powerful leader of the whole Earth: The wheels of his chariot can move anywhere. It was said that, after his death, a chakravartin would be able to sign his name on a hallowed mountain made of pure gold in heaven; this mount, Sumeru, is so beautiful it makes Mount Everest look pathetic. Hearing this, the chakravartin looked forward to death, but wondered where the fun was in signing his name if no one could watch him? He ordered his entire kingdom to kill themselves upon his death, so he could have an audience.

When he dies, he goes up to the gates of heaven with all his kingdom in tow—queens, courtiers, citizens—and is greeted by a gatekeeper, who orders him to leave everyone at the gate. The chakravartin is confused and irritated, but the gatekeeper promises him that he would prefer this upon seeing the mountain. The gatekeeper tells him that every chakravartin has brought a huge number of people with him and every chakravartin who heeded his advice has been grateful for it. So the chakravartin follows the gatekeeper, leaving his posse at the gate. Upon reaching the golden mountain, it is indeed better than anything he imagined. The gatekeeper hands him a special pen to sign his name, but as the chakravartin approaches, he sees the golden mountain is covered with names. There is no space to write.

He is humbled by this—he'd believed himself to be special in reaching this point, only to find that millions of people have been here before him. Then the caretaker of the mountain tells him that the only way to sign his name is to erase another name. Osho writes that, upon hearing this, "The whole joy was gone, the whole excitement was gone . . . ." The chakravartin said to the man, "It just means somebody else will come tomorrow and he will erase my name." The mountain caretaker confirms this is indeed the case; they have to do so, or there isn't enough space. The chakravartin refuses to sign—seeing the pointlessness of it all—and promises to go back to the gate, where, instead of bragging, he shares the wisdom of what he has seen.

I'm telling this story because social media is a powerful challenge for our ego. Many use it to look good and therefore feel good, thrilled to have an audience that they can brag to, similar to the chakravartin wanting to sign his name on the golden mountain. This is further amplified by the dopamine-flavored reward of social validation: notifications.

This is how social media becomes addictive: We get a little hit—not quite enough to satisfy—and we keep going back for more. Have you ever found yourself on the feedback merry-go-round, checking Instagram, then Facebook, then Twitter, around and around, jabbing the refresh button again, and again, and again? Hours of the day can be lost on the online carousel. At its worst, the carousel becomes toxic—especially when we don't get the attention we crave—or we compare ourselves to others, whom we believe are getting the attention and happiness we don't or can't have. We feel less worthy, our lives lacking.

Social media activity is not a symbol of your worth. It's not a substitute for a social life, or face-to-face contact (as anyone in a long-distance relationship will tell you). Neither does it offer a true representation of someone's life or even their true character. Technology has evolved more rapidly than our social skills can keep up with. The power of social media also threatens our ability to develop genuine self-awareness and, especially challenging for teenagers, the chance to develop a balanced, realistic self-image and acceptance. Once we are alert to and self-protective against this, we can use these tools in the reverse: enhancing our communication skills, learning how to build healthy relationships.

Now, more people than ever have public platforms to share their work, their creativity, opinions, thoughts, and feelings. We now see and hear the millions of voices (and smartphones) raised against societal, economic, political, or sexual oppression. With this, we see a huge cultural shift toward redefining and policing unacceptable behavior, both on- and offline. That's where social media offers us real value, affording us a level of insight into the way we act, individually, as members of a community, and as humans in the world, who can spark important real-life conversations, leading to sweeping social change and progress.

Building Relationships in the Community

The most obvious point that everyone misses is that you get back what you put out there, in terms of emotional content. The way people respond to you is a reflection of what you're communicating. We know this instinctively—when we meet someone happy, we start to feel uplifted and share happy memories and thoughts with them. When someone starts telling us a story full of anger, we start to feel angry too. Human beings mirror each other. It takes a large degree of self-awareness to remain in your own emotional state rather than latch on to someone else's.

What this means is, if you post "angry" content online, you will likely receive anger back. Sometimes this will be from a follower sharing your anger, but sometimes it will be from someone angry with you. That's perfectly okay, but if you don't want to handle anger, try adjusting your language and lowering the emotional temperature of your posts. Similarly, more positive posts generate positive responses. You won't always know whether someone is pleased with what you shared, but it might be someone happy about something else entirely who taps into your shared emotion at that moment—or maybe a friend who is just happy you're there.

All this being said, you can share whatever you want— just share *consciously*. Notice how your posts affect how you are received online and experiment. If you don't agree with a post, and you usually just nod along and ignore it, tell someone you don't agree. See how that feels. See how they respond.

Paradoxically, though it certainly enables us to edit ourselves, social media is also a way to be more *you*— to find your voice and to share yourself with others. See what happens when you say something a little different. Be vulnerable. Make friends with people, tell them when you enjoy their posts, let them know if something was valuable to you and how it affected you. Maybe even send them a private message. If you find you are regularly communicating well with someone, arrange to meet in real life. Join online groups that match your interests and add your opinion to the conversation. Remember also that it can be educational to connect with people who have different viewpoints. Perhaps you'll learn something!

I'm lucky enough not to get many nasty comments, but when I do (and if I'm in the right headspace), I always try to respond with kindness and curiosity. Ask questions. What do they really mean by their words? Most people are never really angry at you; often there is something else going on in their life causing this upset, and you've gotten caught in the crossfire. The opportunity to be heard can swiftly neutralize their anger.

There are caveats to this. The first is that it's fine to be curious, but if someone's repeated negativity or posts bring you down, and/or they become abusive, you don't have to stay connected with them or respond to their communications. I will say that if you generate enough loving feeling in your community, people will support you, even if there are others who choose to send abuse.

Try your best to avoid firing off angry posts in the heat of the moment. Knee-jerk reactions are inevitable at times—everyone has triggers. However, a good maxim I used when I was teaching social media management is: "Don't post when you're pissed off." We lose awareness at these times and can end up inscribing a fleeting emotion on the stone tablet of the internet, a place where (terrifyingly) everything is permanently accessible.

At a distance, we can divorce ourselves from reality and forget that there *are* others (with very real feelings) whom we can easily harm in the supposed "echo chambers" into which we shout. Similarly, we can be hurt and shamed when this happens to us. We want to engage, but we struggle to do it in a way that doesn't sound like an attack; it's a good idea to privately message people. It takes the heat out of the communication and shows that we are trying to engage and understand them, not publicly humiliate them. This can allow us to learn and potentially teach someone about our perspective. Ideally, we find validity in both, but if we do not, at least we maximize the opportunity to grow in understanding.

When Social Media Becomes Harmful

When does social media stop becoming a useful exercise in communication and observation—an enjoyable way to catch up with friends—and instead start taking away from and not adding to your life? When not going on it makes you feel uncomfortable. It is now a habit and a distraction, sapping energy from you, maybe even making you feel isolated and lonely (more on this later).

Some of us, without realizing it, end up in a semi-abusive relationship with our phones. We rely on social media notifications for validation and to give us a feeling of accomplishment or activity. We check for them first thing in the morning and last thing at night; we stay on apps longer than we wanted to and lose hours scrolling mindlessly to feed a feeling we didn't even realize we had. We can't sleep; our head's buzzing. If you find yourself in a social media loop (check Twitter: nothing happening; move on to Facebook: not much; on to Instagram: check again—and back around again), then it's likely something is going on that isn't so healthy.

I remember having a little bit of an addiction to social media while working as a journalist. I would spend hours on Twitter in the evening, pretending to myself that it was for work, when really it was just because I didn't quite know what to do with myself. I began to notice that I picked up my phone to check social media whenever I had an uncomfortable feeling. I didn't want to leave my phone outside of the bedroom at night. Social media became another way I was avoiding being with myself, and on top of that, it was fragmenting my attention even further, making it even harder to plan what I wanted to do with my free time.

If any of this sounds like you, there are some really easy, simple changes you can make to wean yourself off social media:

★ Do not make it the first thing you check in the morning.

★ Make a promise to yourself that you will have your first hot drink of the day, take a few breaths, and give yourself some space before you start filling up on it again.

★ Give yourself a social media curfew. You can make a ritual out of it. At 10 p.m., lovingly switch off your phone and put it in a little box to sleep. Let yourself uncurl out of the day without fighting it with screen time.

★ Only check it a maximum of three times a day. The benefit of this is you'll have much more to see when you do check in.

★ Turn off notifications. If need be, remove the apps from your phone. You can also put your phone in grayscale, which turns everything black and white and removes the desire to stay on it very long as it's far less attractive and stimulating.

Social media is a wonderful way to learn about the world and about how humans communicate, to build communities, and to stay connected. But it's a very poor compensation for a life lived offline, and the relationships and communities we build as physical beings, not digital ones.

Where You Live

There's one community you're part of by default, and that is the people who live where you live. It seems a bit nostalgic to talk of local community these days, what with an increase in renting, jobs becoming more mobile, greater migration, and people seeking refugee status. Certainly this idea of a strong community made up of the same group of people who share a permanent space they call home is changing. There are 258 million people living in a country that is not their own, according to a 2017 UN report.

On top of that, we often work far away from where we live, our friends live on the other side of town, and our homes become nothing more than accommodation: places where we eat and sleep (until we retire). How much time do you have to spend somewhere before a location becomes local? And how much longer than that before you describe yourself as "a local"?

It's not really about time. It's about commitment. The two are interconnected, though. When everyone seems to be simply passing through, and even you yourself don't know how long you'll be living in a certain locale, investing time and energy in a place—getting to know the people around you or what's happening in your neighborhood— seems a little precocious. I get it—taking good care of your immediate surroundings when no one else seems to bother, or contributing to maintenance or upkeep when you're barely ever there, seems like a fool's errand. Making new friends and investigating what's going on in a new place feels scary: "I hate small talk—what if the neighbors are weird? Then I'll have to say hi to weirdos for the rest of my life."

The result of having an inner monologue like this? Loneliness. Either for you or for the people around you.

And loneliness is a killer. I could quote stats at you (extreme loneliness increases a person's chances of premature death by 14 percent according to one study), but frankly, we all know how awful feeling lonely is.[30] Isolation in crowds can creep up on us slowly. We don't register how disconnected we are in our homes until we get locked out and realize we don't know anyone we'd feel comfortable having a cup of coffee with until the locksmith arrives.

The purpose of this section is to explain why it's worth giving a f★★k about where you live, taking part in local activities, and getting to know the people close by. Even if you don't feel like it, even if you don't think you'll be living there long, and even if you think your street does not contain "your sort of people"—even if you think no one is interested. Let's stop our world from being full of passing ghosts attached to their phones instead of the space and people around them.

You're Affecting and Affected by Your Local Community, Even if You Don't Realize It

At the end of the nineteenth century, a handsome Frenchman was conducting research into forensics in Lyon, in the first CSI laboratory in the world, for which he had fought hard with the local police department to set up. His name was Dr. Edmond Locard, and he became known as the Sherlock Holmes of France.

He formulated one of the basic principles of forensic science, known as Locard's exchange principle, also known as "every contact leaves a trace." He asserted something that is now held as gospel in forensics: Whatever or wherever someone has been, if there has been contact, they will have left something behind. If a burglar has been in your house, they will have left something behind. If a murder has been committed, there has been some exchange of forensic material. In every contact between people and place, from person to person, something is left behind. It might be invisible to the naked eye, but that doesn't mean it's not there.

Let's think about what this means for the places where we live. If, even on crime scenes, where a perpetrator spends only a short period of time and wants to wipe his imprint away, an exchange can be found, then the impact we leave on where we live, even if it is somewhere we wouldn't call home, could be phenomenal in comparison.

If everywhere we rest for a while is affected by us in some way or another, then we have options: Do you want to be the sort of person who, when they come into contact with a place, makes it better? Or do you want to make it worse? Whatever happens, you're leaving a trace—it doesn't matter how long you stay there for. So take control of that trace. Be part of something in a good way. Actually "live" in your local community.

There's knowing this cognitively, and then there's feeling it. Especially when a place still feels foreign and strange to you. I call it having alien eyes. Alien eyes make you feel under attack. It's that disorienting feeling when you get out of the airport and worry that people are going to mug you, the taxi driver is overcharging you, or the rented apartment feels cold and actively hostile, like it actually wants you to feel lonely. The revolting picture on the wall of the kitchen feels like a personal attack.

Luckily, alien eyes are easily cured. The smallest act can change all this and have you feel part of a place—choosing to pick up a piece of litter and put it in the bin, smiling at someone on the street, saying hi to the person having coffee next to you, offering to carry someone's shopping bags if they are struggling. I now make it my business to generate as much "place karma" as possible; leave the places you stay for a while as good or better off than you found them.

Let Community Work You

It works both ways. This contact between us and a community is an exchange—we affect the community and the community affects us. I believe we absorb a little bit of the places we go and the people we see. If we are influenced by our surroundings no matter what, it makes sense that we become more consciously part of that process so that we can make sure the exchange is a positive one. We gain all the benefits of community as part of that trade between ourselves and our physical environment.

Some people find the idea of local community incredibly suffocating—they prefer the anonymity and perceived freedom that accompanies independence. I'd argue the opposite: How much more free do you feel if you know you have an entire tribe of support on your doorstep? I'm not denying that it can be a challenge to maintain your selfhood, assert your boundaries and not be swayed by worries about the judgment of others in community—but being able to navigate this is an essential part of becoming an adult. Peer pressure and compliance are real, but the price for avoiding these is isolation. Meanwhile, judgment always says more about the person doing the judging than the judged.

It can feel incredibly freeing, too, to discover different parts of yourself: how it's possible to relate to different people, learn new skills, and have a pool of people to call on to ask for advice.

Be a member of a number of different communities, so that you can know that the flavor of one group isn't necessarily the same as another and that's okay. Use them to bring out different sides of you. Know that different communities with their different priorities can help you discover how you feel about certain ways of living. It's good to be able to hang out in different places, with different people, depending on how you feel that day. Pick and choose the parts that suit you, and leave the rest.

Finding and Building Communities

Sometimes we move somewhere where there is already a thriving and active community spirit; it's just a case of finding it. If it's not obvious through an internet search, try typing some relevant search terms into Facebook to look for groups.

If you've still come up empty-handed, then check bulletin boards, or ask people who work locally if they know where you can find out what's going on in the area. Go to the local park and speak with dog owners—usually they know a lot about the area simply because they are out walking the streets and the grassy areas a lot. Churches or synagogues, temples or mosques, also usually have open events for members of the local community. Keep an open mind. Practice being welcoming and approachable. Assume people want to connect until they tell you they don't. Most people are dying for someone to be interested in what they have to say.

Sometimes we might not be able to find a group that suits our needs. That's okay. Belonging is not always a feeling we're born with; it's something we occasionally have to work at. That's when you can set up your own little community.

Life coach Caoilfhionn Nic Conmara brought together a tribe of women for sisterhood brunches after moving from Dublin to London. Every month this group meets at each other's houses, invites new friends they want to introduce to the group, shares food, and then goes and does something local to the area. It's a way of meeting new people, expanding friendship circles, and bonding with women in a friendly, sober, noncompetitive environment.

"When I was feeling lonely last year, I made it my goal to meet as many new people as possible and make a tribe of friends around me," she tells me. "Often when I was feeling especially vulnerable and lonely, I'd ring people up and share how I was feeling, and the resounding answer was always, 'OMG, me, too, London is a lonely town, we all struggle to feel like we fit in.'" She goes on, "Realizing that everybody gets lonely in this city, helped spur me on to organize brunches and events with all my disparate friends, in the hope to build a tribe."

Caoilfhionn Nic Conmara chose women because "Many of my female friends were upset at the dearth of deep female friendships and sisterhood. I wanted all of my female friends to become friends and support each other."

If you want to build your own mini-tribe, or start a gathering in your area, these seven ingredients are helpful in sustaining a community. From my own experience, a well-bonded group that supports its members will always observe these precepts:

★ **A clear and compelling reason for coming together.**
The intention of the group is an important statement and something everyone in the group should know and identify with. It should include a "what" and a "why." This is the shared bond—whether it's picking up litter and making the local area tidier, or a book group discussing a certain genre of literature to learn more, or even a weight-loss group, where people come together to support each other as they get fitter. There may be other benefits (for example, making new friends), but the main intention should be simple and persuasive. This indicates to possible new members why they might want to join and also reminds people already in the community why they are there—for those days when you don't feel like turning up to choir practice or helping pick up litter.

★ **Make it inclusive.** Choosing to set up a group defined solely by who is not allowed in is the equivalent of making friends to help you build a shrine to your own insecurities. The covert way of doing this is making the barrier to entering the community so difficult that it dissuades people from joining. Chill out. Encourage people to invite their friends. Be welcoming. Encourage members to befriend each other. Set up a buddy system for new people so they have a point of contact. Foster an environment where everyone is greeted as if they were a film star or a long-lost friend. There are not enough hugs and smiles in this world; there's no need to be standoffish and corporate in community.

★ **Arrange regular physical meet-ups.** Virtual communities are great, but they pale in comparison to in-the-flesh meetings. Set a date and time (say, the first Saturday of every month), and stick to it. Make it convenient for the group you're in; if childcare is an issue, you might want to choose a different day, for example. Regular dates and times allows people to plan to be there. Check in with people before to ask if they will be able to make it, to jog their memories. Have an online presence, to allow people to communicate in between and build connection. WhatsApp threads or Facebook groups are great for this.

★ **Set up a structure that reinforces inclusivity.** Icebreakers work. Make sure you get everyone's voice in the room early on or have a system that allows everyone who wants to be heard to be. If the group is small enough, do a round of names or introductions. For larger groups, you might want to give out name badges (it's hard to remember, and it's embarrassing to keep asking). If possible, provide context on who knows whom or how long they've been a member—it's easy to feel like the odd one out. Information can be a way for people to pick up personal conversations later.

★ **Have guidelines, community rules, and etiquette.** Community guidelines help people feel safe so that they feel they can reveal themselves (for example, a confidentiality or no-judgment rule) and also reaffirm the purpose of the group. Usually the etiquette is there for a reason. For example, in hot yoga, you are asked not to leave the room so that you stay in the zone and don't disturb others. In my orgasmic meditation women's group, where we talk about being sexual as women, they ask us not to indulge in one-downmanship—if one person has had a bad week, it doesn't mean we all need to play down our achievements or happy experiences in order to try to make them feel better. It's something that women often do, so they pre-warn us in order to counter that tendency we have toward sympathetic modesty. These guidelines aren't "enforceable" as such; they are often just rails to direct the community toward more effective action.

★ **Encourage greater and greater involvement.** It's a good idea if you can in some way share different roles around the group so that one week one person is leading, and another week someone else is. It not only feels "fair" and gives people different experiences, but it also lets everyone become more invested in the community. It also stops a false hierarchy from developing among older members of the group and the running of the community from becoming onerous if left to one or two people. If the group expands in numbers, establishing a committee might be the way forward—you could even make the committee a rolling one. Donations or other contributions can also help people invest more—putting money into something is one way people come to feel part of it.

★ **Make it fun.** No one wants to take part in something that becomes a chore—too restrictive or overly dogmatic. Bring joy into the group, even if it's serious. Encourage socializing before and after events and ties between members. With many communities I've been a part of, I've signed up for one thing and ended up coming back again and again for the friends I've made and the fun it is to hang out together.

The amazing thing about building a community where you live is that you always have a baseline interest in common to build on: your shared location. That sounds great, but actually there's nothing like close contact to produce friction. Take it as a given; you're annoying at times and your neighbors are going to be annoying at times. The more things you have in common, the more annoying they'll be. (There's nothing like sharing a front door to dramatically increase how objectively awful someone is; it's truly fascinating.) There will be times when you are comforted only by the realization that you are also as annoying to them as they are to you.

There's always a way through, and it's in both your interests to find it. When you do, the rewards for navigating that tough situation will be greater too. In my experience, the more possessive you are, the more problems you're going to have. Step back. Caring here does not mean controlling or getting fixated; it means wanting to make things better.

The best thing about caring in community is that it is contagious. There's a woman on my street who, simply because she likes gardening, has dug up around the trees in our little cul-de-sac and planted all kinds of flowers. Now we have daffodils on our road instead of old fried-chicken bones and weeds and cigarette butts. Every time I see these flowers, it's a reminder to me that anything we do that improves an environment for us also has an impact on others that extends beyond the action itself. They work as an inspiration or an invitation for us all to do a little to make where we live that much brighter. I'm grateful to her not just for making our two streets look prettier but for reminding me to care.

Infinity
and Beyond

GIVE A F**K
ABOUT INFINITY
AND BEYOND

Caring about the wider world used to feel totally overwhelming for me. Chaotic, unmanageable, and exhausting. Most of the time it was out of my range to care about anything other than whatever current turbulence was running my life and absorbing my attention. There were some occasional moments in the small hours between sleeping and waking when bigger questions about the world and who I was, in a macro, more magical sense, would germinate in my dreamy mind, but I would forget them promptly upon waking up and get to work, instead being busy with the drama du jour.

My lack of interest in the world bothered me a bit, but I put it down to simply being a bit of a self-absorbed person, one of the many flawed, egocentric humans I saw in the world who couldn't give much of a f**k outside their own sphere. Even their posts on Facebook professing altruism were nothing more than a performance of goodness. I was a very cynical human, and I saw vanity, ignorance, anger, and pride all around me. I didn't want to give a f**k because I thought it was hopeless and I thought it wasn't worth it.

I have come to realize I was wrong to judge myself in this way, and I was wrong about the nature of humanity. I fundamentally do care about this planet and had the desire to care even back then—it's just that I had some house-keeping to do on myself before that was possible. I think a lot of us feel this way, to a certain extent, and we could be a bit more compassionate with each other while we go through that process.

The reason I was so tense and anxious about the world was that the way I felt about myself was off, my relationships with other people were disconnected, and I had no community. Essentially, how I felt about myself mirrored my general confusion and resentment toward the universe and all that was in it. If I had told myself back then that I could care so actively about the world and it could feel glorious, I would have thought it impossible. That's why this section is last, after the advice about how to give a f**k about relating to yourself and others, because, in St. Francis of Assisi's words, "Start by doing what's necessary, then do what's possible, and suddenly you are doing the impossible."

It's not about perfection—totally nailing the self-love, being a distinguished boundary setter, and becoming hailed as a community leader before you start to relate consciously to the wider world (although having a strong platform of self-care and friends and feeling part of something will help anchor you on this journey). What we believe about the world and our place within it will inform how we behave in all those other areas, and these in turn will affect how we relate to the wider world.

When I talk about the wider world, I'm looking at the bigger-picture things that influence our everyday lives but that we rarely stop and consider thoughtfully. Some are more tangible—like the news and money. Others are more abstract and philosophical—like what our purpose is or where we find meaning. What we think about love, pain, and humanity—our worldview. All of these things are incredibly important to give a f★★k about—and to investigate why they are important to us. Then we can adjust our relationship to them to serve us and the world better.

First, the news—we watch it, read it, listen to it, and discuss topics that come up, but short of straightforward complaining, we don't actually think about why we care about the news or what it gives us. And because we don't do that, we can't examine how to give a f★★k about it in such a way that we aren't stuck between despair and anger at the media and instead can be provided with a news service that does what it is meant to: illuminate global and local issues that are important, in an interesting and informative way.

Similarly, we exchange money every day, but how many of us stop and think about our relationship to money itself and how it might be holding us back? Holding us back from making more, holding us back from valuing ourselves and our services, holding us back from making friends (maybe ones who aren't in the same financial bracket), holding us back from pitching for great things in front of great people? Most of us do care about money, but in a way that only serves to dishonor ourselves and others. Like news, we have a habit of making it too important or disconnecting from it altogether. Money is a taboo topic; let's drag it out from under the jealous dragon and examine our attitudes to it so that we can be free and generous in our financial dealings, rather than tight, defensive, and constrained.

Because money and news are visible, loud presences in our lives, it may seem like they have more impact on who we are and what we do than the more ephemeral matters of finding a sense of purpose and nurturing a positive worldview. However, on a subterranean level, these big questions inform everything we think, feel, and do. They direct our lives, almost invisibly, from the very depths of us. It may seem daunting to ask ourselves how we feel about such deep subjects, especially when no answers seem immediately forthcoming. It's true—some people have made investigating these questions their life's work. However, just being willing to sit with these topics is a process that lets us peel back layers of conditioning and fear, many of which have long outgrown their use, so that we can get in touch with the beauty that's deep within us.

There's this curious thing about examining how we feel about the wider world—it puts us more in touch with the core of who we really are, which then helps us reconnect with the wider world in a way that's more authentic, present, invested, and enjoyable. That's when caring starts to feel good, almost automatic—an effortless part of being, fundamental to who you are. Plugging into this bigger picture, we feel connected to ourselves, to people around us, to the community we live in, and to the world. Giving a f★★k about the wider world is really just a beautiful way to care for yourself.

The News

Before I tell you why you need to care about the news, let me declare my bias. I am a former full-time member of the mainstream media (MSM). I care deeply about news and about the way people engage with it. I've spent most of the last decade trying (quite successfully, ultimately) to get people to read, listen to, and watch the news that my colleagues and I produce. Persuading people to engage with and value the news they consume is vital to ensuring its proper production, and properly produced news can change the world.

Saying that, I also know there is such a thing as caring too much—or caring "unhealthily" about the news. I stopped working in the news not only because it exposed me to a boiling cauldron of pain, fear, and constant disaster but also because I could feel it cause ripples of trauma across social media, an avalanche of negative news affecting people's emotional state. I know an awful lot about the effects of overconsumption of news—if you're looking for an expert on how to relate to current affairs in a way that will damage your mental health, I'm your woman. That's why caring about the news is not enough—it's *how* you care about it that counts.

I also left current affairs because I dislike the way the current media model operates, perhaps just as much as those who moan about the news online every day.

Fundamentally, though, I can see how much excellent news reporting there is—despite the difficult conditions—and I'm continually grateful for being able to access information about the world around me in real time, from sources that I (more or less) trust. I'm not denying there are problems. The media isn't perfect, but the solution is not to switch off and care less; it's to care more.

We need to care about the news for five crucial reasons: to find out what's going on that affects us (if we want to live in this world, it's helpful to know what's going on in it); to make a change and have impact; to stretch our perspective and introduce us to new ideas; to connect with others and feel part of the whole; and to learn from mistakes.

"Hear Ye, Hear Ye"

Bulletins, newspapers, and push updates have a very basic practical function, a bit like the town crier of old. The media provides a shared space where issues that affect us can be raised and discussed. Where else can you make announcements or let people know what's going on? Sure, we can send people letters, or do group texts, but what if you don't have that information? How do you get a message out?

Lots of newspapers have "gazette" in the
title because the first Venetian newspapers,
in the sixteenth century, cost one
gazzetta—a Venetian coin.

It's no good howling at the moon when something happens if you've disengaged with all the discussions leading up to it. In fact, when changes are not adequately publicized, people suffer adversely. In some countries, governments restrict press freedom, controlling the flow of information to repress their people. This is one role that the news plays in our lives—it serves as a kind of information forum, where we can check in and see what is happening that may affect us or people we love. No one wants to eat a horse-meat lasagna if they don't need to.

Additionally, the pressure of publicity can force change—when things are dragged into the light, people can come together against it. Before Edward Snowden leaked documents about the NSA collecting data, causing a worldwide scandal, it wasn't known that the U.S. government had been mass monitoring global communications. It was even reported that Angela Merkel's cell phone had been monitored—leading to the German chancellor calling President Barack Obama and telling him (according to reports) that "spying among friends is never acceptable." A recent example of publicity forcing change in the U.K. is the Windrush scandal—the treatment of people who arrived from the Caribbean between 1948 and

1970, who were threatened with deportation (and, in some cases, actually deported) in error due to new bureaucratic rules designed to deter other immigrants in 2012. Their appalling treatment had been happening for years without a national uproar. Caribbean leaders had complained to the U.K. government about these enforced deportations of older people who had lived legally in the country, paying taxes for over fifty years, only to be put on a plane to Jamaica in their seventies. It wasn't until fresh cases were reported in the press, embarrassing the Home Office and fueling public anger, that changes began to be made to benefit these citizens.

The news explodes our perspective—not only might we hear of events in our local area that otherwise we wouldn't hear about, of things that might interest or affect us, but also we hear of issues in places we may never visit.

The world continually challenges our imagination with its possibilities, and when it's not priests, drug dealers, or shamans bending our reality, then it's journalists who often wear the winged sandals, reporting facts stranger than fiction. The metaphor "a black swan" was used in Europe (as far back as the Roman poet Juvenal) to mean something that didn't exist. Which was all lovely and clever and satirical until Europeans began to settle in Australia and discovered that black swans did in fact exist. How embarrassing. If only there had been CNN!

I'm being facetious. The color of swans may not impact our lives so much, but this term has been repopularized by Nassim Nicholas Taleb in his book, *The Black Swan:*

The Impact of the Highly Improbable, to describe things that we can't predict because they are unlike our previous experiences.[31] There are still a lot of questions about the world that we have yet to answer, both individually and collectively. We don't even know what to google because we have no reference point for it. And yet, if we don't acknowledge them, or seek to uncover them, they can derail us. Reading the news is one way we can begin to familiarize ourselves with the unexpected, and broaden our own experience of the world so that we have more data to base our decisions on, adjusting our relationship to the world and widening our perspectives.

We find out about space travel, electric cars, and kings under parking lots. We are told of volcanoes erupting, of plane crashes, of cougar attacks, of refugee camps, of Ebola and Zika. We hear about what's captivating conversation in countries besides our own—of crimes that have sent shockwaves through international cultures—and we face the headlines that affect our local communities too. The news tells us of things that immediately concern and affect us, and things that appear not to. It illuminates the differences between cultures and also allows us to see our shared humanity, if we allow it. Grief looks the same on faces the world over, even if mourning takes a different ritual form. News allows us to connect with others, both near and far, and helps us feel connected to the whole. This happens on a very visceral level in coffee shops—if people are discussing the weather, then they're talking about something in the news. It's something we share and use to connect.

Media reporting influences our lives, no matter how far away it is; the headlines affect the beliefs and behaviors of those around us, the economy, and the emotional temperature of society. It is almost impossible to remain in our own bubble anymore—it would mean avoiding the internet, social media, and newsstands and only coming into contact with people who do the same. We live and operate in a space shared with others, who are also affected by the news—the markets and our moods are subtly shifting all the time. What's reported becomes part of our collective landscape whether we like it or not.

In short, Toto, not only are we are not in Kansas anymore, but whatever happens in Munchkinland is going to affect Aunt Em and Uncle Henry back home, as well as impact the trees in the Haunted Forest and quite possibly blow up Emerald City too. Globalization is here, and it doesn't give a f**k if you want to elect Trump or vote for Brexit. We are connected now, and it will take the heart, courage, and brains of all of us to see this one through.

The best possible scenario is that we all learn from each other, developing respect, love, and cooperation. The worst possible scenario is that we don't—and if one country goes down, we all go down in the ensuing tornado. The news is a bit like monogamy or democracy: It's not ideal and it fails us repeatedly, but for most of us, it's marginally better than the alternative, which is not knowing a damn thing and completely disengaging with the world and what it's currently reading, watching, and talking about.

Knowing what's going on out there allows us to see and feel opportunities to care more. Places where our skills might be needed for what interests us—there might even be a place where you see how you can set up a business or offer a service. News organizations are great for alerting us to top-level information—it is up to us what we do next at ground level. Discover an event where people are talking about an issue. Sign up. Buy a book. Embrace the crazy and see if there's hidden genius there. Learn from the history, the mistakes, what came before the reported event, and why people think the way they do. News is not necessarily only top-level—it's just what is new. There's always going to be more to it than can be contained in the latest update.

What's Wrong with the News

My experience of people who criticize the media in its entirety is that they have a fundamental misunderstanding of how the news is forced to operate and its reliance on the audience to direct its output. You might as well criticize capitalism or humanity, or, dare I say it, the nature of reality.

The way the news is delivered is in flux right now. No one knows more than the media the difficulty with the current model. The idea that you could report "the facts" as they happen, globally, twenty-four hours a day, seven days a week, on demand, for free, with excellent visual data and succinct analysis, is a problematic one at best. Philosophers and historians still clash over what the truth is, but yes, sure, a 35-year-old reporter, with a camera, in a war zone, is definitely going to be able to get to the bottom of it by 6 p.m. so it can make the show.

Of course, there's a limit to what's knowable, but there are some facts that are beyond dispute too. That doesn't mean we should stop engaging with the news—it just means we need to adjust our relationship to it. To see it as the gateway to greater knowledge, rather than reading headlines as signs saying "the truth stops here," with flashing arrows to the copy underneath.

There is a lot wrong with the news and journalists, but Lord, audiences like to moan about things journalists can't control. Sometimes the feedback is helpful: when someone points out an inaccuracy or that some phrasing in a headline or article was poor. But you really can't please everyone. In my experience, sometimes people would be so angry that the BBC wasn't reporting something properly (we were, they just couldn't find it up high enough on the website) or wasn't reporting it at all (we were trying to—there was no conspiracy, we would be aware of it, and we were merely trying to check it was true or that the source was legitimate and worth trusting). Or maybe their "story" just wasn't sufficiently important to the nation— people simply didn't care enough.

That's the thing audiences don't understand. We report what *you* want to hear about, what you share, and what you read—even more these days, because we have the data on what is popular. Even more so because of the way algorithms work, because peer-reviewed news is now the way we consume, so the most-read stories become even more read.

Stop reading the news because you're bored—or you'll only read the most entertaining, shocking, titillating, curious pieces with the silly headlines that misrepresent the serious article. Don't share it to show how silly it is.

Do not read what you do not want produced. Do not share articles you think are fundamentally awful. Even screenshots. Don't joke about them.

Stop making awful people famous because you love to position yourself in opposition to them, either to laugh at them or to show people that you're trustworthy and A Good Person. It is an attention economy online—the free news market only wants eyeballs. Stop giving attention to things you don't like and don't want. (That's a good philosophy for life, not just for news.)

Editors try not to cater to the lowest common denominator, but audiences don't often help. We'll spend time and money trying to make you read something about Yemen, but if you don't read it or share it, we'll stop investing, until someone pipes up and makes a case for why we should do it anyway. If you want news coverage, get a campaign group together and make a pact to share everything on it. Get Facebook groups, Twitter lists, numbers. Get good pictures. Then journalists will start covering all your issues. That is how it works. It's not about people getting the media they deserve; it's that people get the media they click on, share, and are willing to pay for.

Buy your news. It might feel a bit chicken and egg: "I hate the media, so why should I pay for it?" But just hang on with the economics for a second. Free online readers are worth so little to publishers that the sheer numbers needed on every article to allow the organization to survive are immense. It means a large volume of articles have to be produced, which means a quick turnaround, which means no time to research or take care. That means attention-grabbing and quick hits and the news you love to hate.

What Bias?

When I worked online, I usually saw about seven main gripes from readers, broadly grouped into "That's not true," "That headline is misleading," "That's not newsworthy," "Why aren't you reporting on [insert other story]?," "Fake news," and "You're biased." Obviously, pointing out whether something is true or not can be helpful. Sometimes a different view on a headline, if it's alienating readers, can be useful feedback too. The newsworthy one is a uselessly subjective complaint that really irritates me because we know as journalists that it's not serious news; we also know from watching our analytics that you're damn well reading it in droves, far above our in-depth reporting on trade tariffs and prison reform.

However, the gripe about bias is one I always think is the most ridiculous, although it's obviously valid and affects all media organizations. It even messes with ones like the BBC that try to offset it with opposing voices and end up overcompensating: allowing people who are simply racist or wrong a large amount of airtime in order to provide "balance." The most I think we can ever do is know and declare our biases as much as possible.

We are all biased: Sometimes we can become conscious of our prejudices, and sometimes we have bias blind spots that, no matter how hard we try, we fail to see. Every reader has bias. Every journalist has bias. Sometimes people shout fake news when they really mean "We do not share the same bias!"

I'm a woman—I'm going to feel more engaged with certain equality issues. I'm white—I'm almost definitely going to have less cultural or emotional investment and even, dare I say it, more implicit bias while reporting on stories that focus on race, compared to someone from another ethnic background (it's why diverse newsrooms are so important). Those are some biases I can work to eradicate or compensate for when I cover certain stories, so that I interview different people with different viewpoints from mine, then have an editor and another editor check and double-check to see if I'm leaking any implicit bias.

Many companies are now training staff about diversity by having an implicit bias test that can assess whether, despite your best intentions, you have some automatic preferences— that check, for example, if you are biased against LGBT people, the obese, the disabled, or people from another race. This is particularly important for those recruiting for the business, as automatic bias can see the most talented people not hired for a role, simply because of their background and the bias of those in HR.

Journalists do the best they can not to let bias affect their work, so they put out only what is closest to objective as possible, but there are always limits. For example, say you are reporting from Iraq but being escorted by the U.S. army—which may be for safety reasons; you can only get detail from a certain viewpoint.

Be curious and caring about this by reading at least three different sources of news—don't just take one article as fact. Be aware that lots of papers use the same wire service—this means that media organizations pay for an independent company to send its journalists out and report back facts. We are all using the same sources sometimes.

If something interests you, it's great to seek out opinion pieces that can help adjust the lens through which you are viewing events. Be aware, though: A compelling writer with a persuasive arguing style does not necessarily a truth-teller make.

Changing Our Relationship

The news poses an almost insurmountable challenge to us. This goes beyond the challenge of absorbing the sheer volume of information available. It's harder than the dilemma of sifting through what is true, what might be true, and what is almost definitely not. It's even more difficult than acknowledging our own individual bias and adjusting the lens through which we observe events unfolding in the world today. The news rocks our sense of certainty and power. It makes us feel insignificant, and it hits us right in that terrible spot where instability and panic overwhelm us: "I don't know," "I didn't know," "I don't understand," and "I have no idea what to do next" are words that no one ever wants to hear, think, or say in the face of catastrophe.

Journalists, analysts, and audiences all fall victim to our fear of the uncertain and the unknowable. And to soothe us, politics and personality step in to fill the gap, sweeping in with a simplistic sound bite for a complex problem. Mark Twain said, "Politicians and diapers must be changed often, and for the same reason." It's probably not entirely fair to say they are full of sh★t, but they are certainly full of fear. Why else would you—how even could you—blame or shame others for getting it wrong or profess to have a solution in the way that most politicians do? Or even front-page headline writers? We are so afraid of the unknown, we'd rather know familiar suffering, pain, blame, and shame. We create one-dimensional villains and flash-in-the-pan heroes. At least we can understand them. At least they are familiar.

Care about the issues. We *need* to care about science, technology, the environment, health, housing, discrimination, conflict, and business—but don't get sidetracked by politics. They may seem inseparable, but they are not. If we stripped away the politics of *how*, most of us could agree on a *what*—a better quality of life, less crime, more peace, less poverty, more wealth, less ignorance, more knowledge, less hate, more love.

Politics peddles how each party or political ethos has one plan for what to do next. Unfortunately, that one plan also comes with an identity and a wholesale philosophy. Sign up for one thing, and you have to sign up for the whole lot. How crazy is that? We'd never have relationships with anyone if we had to go about our personal lives that way.

"Oh, I can only like you if I like everything about you. Sorry, I'm not going to agree with you on this, because if I agree with you on this, I have to agree with you on everything." It's madness. Terrible people have good ideas. Good people have terrible ideas. It doesn't have to turn into a competition about who is responsible and who is the worst—rather, let's look at the problem and be open to solutions, even if the solutions are complicated and demand nuance. Apologies if it's not as good a story.

All of this is to say, we can be better than backseat drivers when it comes to the news. Instead of loudly grumbling to the other passengers about how crappy the driver is, see if he's taking you where you want to go. If not, start googling better directions and decide where you want to end up. Read longer pieces. Get curious. Learn about the issue, talk to people who know about the issue, get informed. Seek areas of agreement rather than gleefully lecturing someone else on how wrong they are. Don't just bitch and carp online about how crappy the media is and how everyone is corrupt. You have more power than you think to shape the way your friends, family, colleagues, and peers feel or think about issues important to you, but if you channel all that passion and provocation into ranting into the abyss of a comments forum, the power is wasted.

Pledges for Good News Reading

★ I will click, read, or share the type of news I want to see more of.

★ I will pay for quality journalism.

★ I will aim for impartiality, reading more than one news source and looking at more than one viewpoint on issues that are important to me.

★ I will investigate and be interested in my own bias.

★ I will share the news I care about.

★ I will not check or read the news more than three times a day.

★ I will connect and share with my friends news that interests me and ask for second opinions.

★ I will remember that there are limits to what the news can provide.

Money

I'm a spiritual person, but I like nice shoes. Free-range eggs cost more, and organic, fair-trade vegetables don't come cheap. I like to buy books, and I am a big fan of further education. I enjoy doing yoga and having coaching and time to do nothing but dance in my pajamas.

All of this is to say that, in my experience, having money is a good thing. Plus, frankly, cheap wine tastes like crap (although you can still have a lot of fun on it).

There is a certain brand of disciple that might pooh-pooh my materialism. Let me clarify: I'm not suggesting you get attached to the expensive hairdresser, fluffy towels, or the Tempur-Pedic mattress—enjoying your life doesn't need to be dependent on any conditions, especially not material ones. I agree that true freedom is not needing the latest edition or the nice yoga mat or the high-speed internet (although trying to work on a Google Doc with a poor connection would make even the Dalai Lama swear, I'd wager). But I enjoy having money, and I like the easy opportunities it gives me to experience certain things in life. Plus, who am I kidding? I enjoy the comfort and the pleasure of it all. I'm an extrovert—the advantages of monkish existence have always been a hard sell to me.

There are, of course, ways to spend your money that are more nourishing than others, and a large bank balance doesn't mean happiness. You're going to feel desperate in a different way if you're isolated or don't have nourishing relationships. There are benefits of having less money, too, and I'll get to those later. However, I'd argue for the general assumption that food, safety, and shelter are basic requirements for profitable human existence, and money helps us get those.

Cash is not the be-all and end-all, but it damn well feels that way if you need it. It's hard to be spiritual if you're in a high-rise apartment with five hungry children and the TV turned up loud to drown out the drug bust next door. "Use the sound of domestic violence to bring you even deeper into the present," said no meditation app ever.

My basic philosophy on money is simple: Having money is useful, and having more of it even more so. Swapping money for goods and services is one way we can access things to improve our lives and those of other people. That's why we should give a f★★k about money.

Most of us do care about it, particularly how much we have, how much other people have, and whether those two amounts match (although we wouldn't admit it, at least not in polite company). Money is so taboo, people would rather talk about death, politics, religion, sex—anything else. In relationships, we sleep with someone before telling them how much we earn. Letting someone touch our genitals is less intimate than letting someone glimpse our bank statement. It's fair to say we have some shame around money.

Perhaps we should, if, as the biblical phrase tells us, "Money is the root of all evil." Unfortunately, however, that is a misquotation that's had us crippled with financial embarrassment for hundreds of years. The actual quote in 1 Timothy 6:10 is: "For the love of money is a root of all kinds of evil." It's not money that's the root of all evil; it's what we end up thinking about money that hurts us, whether we're rich or poor, or a member of the smug-as-hell middle classes.

Problem is, if we won't talk about or look at it, we can't really begin to understand how we relate to it and adjust those beliefs to serve us better. Most people think and care about money in such a way that it doesn't help them make it, spend it, donate it, or build connections with people who have more or less money than them.

Money, in and of itself, is incredibly useless. In the past, you could exchange your bank note for actual gold, which, by the way, is also pretty useless. Tried washing your hair with gold? Making pasta with gold? Driving to town on some gold? However, now you can't even make that exchange. A bank note is simply an IOU from the treasury. It's plastic and metal. Money is only valuable as long as we all agree that it is.

And we do agree on that: Money is one of the ways we signify value in our society. It's not the only way, though— so don't get too sidetracked equating price with value, especially because money means different things to different people. The same amount of physical cash can be considered expensive or cheap depending on the relative importance of the goods or service it is exchanged for in one person's perception. Other ways we show value can be with the quality of our attention; sharing our skills, time, and trust with others; by qualifications; and through respect and love. For some people, taking the time to teach someone something would be a far greater compliment than paying them a lump sum. It's very personal; we all make money mean different things.

The truth is, the amount of money you have in your bank account means … that is how much money you have in your bank account. It does not mean you have no talent, no power, no resources, or no worth. You, as a human being, don't lose or gain anything in terms of intrinsic value depending on how much money you have. We seem to forget that, though, and associate money with lots of different connotations that don't benefit us.

Check How Many of These You Agree With

★ Richer people are less generous with their money.

★ Poorer people are more loving.

★ Richer people are stuck up.

★ Richer people are better educated.

★ Poorer people haven't made the most of their opportunities.

★ Richer people haven't experienced life.

★ Rich people don't understand what it is like to be poor.

★ Poorer people have more appreciation for things.

★ Richer people are just lucky.

★ Richer people are a slave to their possessions.

★ Life has been unfair to poor people.

★ Rich people don't understand the meaning of life.

★ I judge how people spend their money.

★ I judge how successful someone is according to how much money they have.

★ I find it uncomfortable hanging out with people who have much more or much less than I have.

★ I wouldn't let anyone see my bank balance.

★ I think people in debt are foolish/irresponsible.

Are you getting a picture of where you stand with money? We heap all this meaning onto rich and poor, but there are so many different, contradictory views about money that it ceases to have any meaning at all, other than what it can buy. Our view on money doesn't even reflect our financial situation—it's not even ours most of the time.

We've inherited our meaning of money from our parents, class, or culture.

Expanding Your Value and Possibilities

A certain mind-set about money can hold us back. If we think "rich" is a dirty word, it will be more difficult to increase our funds. There's going to be a ceiling—a certain amount that we think is "a lot of money"—where we unconsciously put the brakes on either charging more, earning more, investing more in ourselves, or spending in a way that gives us joy. A place where we think "that's too much to ask," lower our prices, or walk away from the thing we really want.

This is not about ripping people off or getting into crippling debt. First things first—make money in a way that brings value to the world. If you don't know how you bring value, go back and read the section on work or consider changing what you do. Wallace D. Wattles puts it well in *The Science of Getting Rich*: "If you are selling any man anything which does not add more to his life than the thing he gives you in exchange, you can afford to stop it. ... Give every man more in use value than you take from him in cost value; then you are adding to the life of the world by every business transaction."[32]

Once you are less shackled to the idea of earning or charging a lot as being somehow shameful, when you are sure of all the nonmonetary value you provide through what you offer, you will feel freer to charge the true price for your service or product. If need be, write a list of all the value you give or contribute to in exchange for the money you charge. For example, if you are a sports coach for children, the obvious value you provide is in teaching children how to play a sport. But there might be other, secondary value, that you provide too: babysitting, getting children into the fresh air, increasing their fitness, nurturing a love of exercise early, and creating fond memories—it might be socializing with other children in a fun environment, or boosting confidence. All of these things are part of the service you offer.

In order to boost your value when negotiating a salary or offering services, try stating a range, where the lowest point is what you actually want. One study by Columbia Business School psychologists found that when job applicants stated a range as their requested salary, where the lowest number was their desired pay, they received significantly higher salaries.[33]

Charge a price that feels scary to ask for. Too many of us undervalue our services in terms of money, then become resentful when we put in the time and effort necessary to do a good job to the standard we want to do it.

We need to provide value to others, to feel valuable to others—it gives us satisfaction and fulfillment as humans—

but we struggle to ask for the money that would allow us to do this without becoming bitter. We're not good at accurately rating how much we should—and could—charge for our time and service. There's such a thing as being reassuringly expensive to a customer—allowing them to realize what they are purchasing has value and that value is recognized by the person they are buying it from.

If you value yourself, and what you offer, you will also spend money investing in improving your offering, which supports other businesses and leads to progress all around. Because what you spend money on is a sign of what you value, investing it in yourself (wisely) is also an act that promotes your own well-being. There's a phrase: Put your money where your mouth is—i.e., back up what you are saying with a tangible investment. I'd go one step further: Put your money where your heart is, or even where you want your heart to be. Spend your money the way someone who loves themselves, or values their life, would. If that means saving for a gym membership, then so be it.

One of the key things here is spending your money on new experiences—ones that promote inner progress. There's something called the hedonic treadmill, which informs this way of spending to promote happiness. Humans adapt very quickly, returning to a relatively stable level of happiness whatever the circumstances—good or bad. That means if you spend an awful lot of money on maintaining a very opulent lifestyle, after a while you will simply get used to it, and it will cease to bring you the contentment it used to.

But if you cut down on the everyday spends, and use that money for new experiences, you'll feel more satisfied.

There's nothing wrong with wanting to be rich so that we can have more experiences in life. Earning money or spending money so that we increase the value of what we can offer the world is not "greedy" or morally wrong. The problem comes when we make being rich a rigid "must" or "should"—that we *have to* earn lots of money. That's when we grip and grasp, getting competitive and scrambling for the goal at any cost. The other trap with accumulating wealth is when we want money to fill some other gap in our psyche that money is poorly suited to satisfy. This is important. If the reason you want a car is a sense of status and power, then you may find a car is not the best way to get that.

Your Dream Budget

See if you can expand your range for what is possible for you—to find out where you are limiting yourself with a belief that you cannot earn more or that the world doesn't value you enough. Gaining money for money's own sake is the goal of a nincompoop. Instead, look at the things you want, in an ideal world: if money were no object. Then attach a price to them. It might look like this:

★ Less anxiety (therapy: $60 a week)
★ More time off (buy vacation days from work: $300)
★ Personal trainer ($60 a week)
★ Massage training course ($400)

The sky's the limit. It doesn't matter that you might be unable to afford these things right now—the important thing is to set a goal for where you want to go. Work out what your yearly income would need to be to afford all of these things. Then you can list what they would give you and others, too, if you were able to get them. For example, more time off means more relaxation, more time spent time with family, a greater sense of love/peace, more time spent with nature, perhaps better relationships with friends, and being more available at work when you are there. Sure, if you just want something because it looks pretty and it's fun, well, leave it on. Just know that is the reason you want it—and hey, maybe there are other ways to give yourself pretty, fun things in life, something you could give yourself now.

The very act of writing down what you want is a brilliant way to get in touch with yourself, and it may give you an impetus to move forward—something to fuel you to charge the uncomfortable price for your services, to look for opportunities to earn money, to ask for a raise. If looking at the budget feels overwhelming, then you may want to go back and write an intermediary list—one that doesn't seem too far off from where you are now but that stretches you.

In the meantime, there are some tangible advantages to be gained, should you find yourself in a position with not as much money as you would prefer. I don't want to go too Pollyanna on you or deny that losing/not having money is stressful, but there are ways to look at being—ahem, less abundant—so that you make the most of it.

Shoestring Living

The primary benefit to having less money is that it is uncomfortable, which means you have to wake up. We live in a comfort-addicted, perfection-obsessed culture, asleep at the wheel as we bump from purchasing one numbing experience to another. We buy to get high—layering the exhilaration of a bargain, or a shiny new acquisition, over a difficult feeling, so we can ignore our inner discomfort.

When you have less money, you have the opportunity to be more aware of the world, simply because you can't afford to buy the same level of distraction. Being forced to sit with that, we learn it is more bearable than we thought. It might be challenging but we can live through it, and it can actually set us free to direct our lives how we want to move forward—rather than simply navigating ourselves away from pain.

By being exposed to your discomfort, you can learn how to work with what is, how to go into an experience fully and enjoy it for what's there, rather than buying things or trying to change it because it feels less than perfect. You have to look for what is right, rather than complain that the people are wrong or the venue is wrong or the clothes are wrong or the food is wrong.

The second benefit to being down on your money luck is the fact that having less automatically puts you in cooperation with other people. You might have to reach out to people: to share experiences because it is cheaper, ask for help, or propose doing something together. What is great about having less money is that you have to get creative. You have to be creative about having the fun you want. Can you work backstage in order to see the concert for free? Can you dog-sit or apartment/house-swap to get free accommodations while on vacation? What do you have of value to sell? What do you have to exchange? What services can you provide for people? Basically, you have to up your hustle game; challenge what you think is possible, challenge what other people think is possible from you, and get as resourceful as you can. You may find you have more than you thought you did.

Having less money is not a prerequisite for waking up to either of these truths, but if you find yourself in hard times, it can focus your mind into such realization. Preferably, we'd all discover this with a decent amount of cash—but we don't, because the way we spend our money doesn't necessarily help us.

Getting Conscious with Money

There was a point in between jobs where I was, shall we say, broke. I was not bringing any money in, and I had deeply underestimated the rate I needed to spend it to live on my own in Central London. The wake-up call for me was exchanging years-old foreign currency from Russia, Thailand, and Europe to get enough money to buy groceries and putting pots and pans on eBay to pay rent on time. I have more tools in my toolkit than lining up at Western Union with a handful of coins ("I'm afraid, madam, that's actually a peso") and more to offer the world than hard-wearing crockery. Sure, prices in my city were high and the media competitive, but if I looked within my circle of influence, I also wasn't paying attention to my finances enough.

I hate the idea of budgeting or "saving" because it makes me think of sitting at home, eating a can of baked beans (or some tuna in brine if I'm lucky), depriving myself of friends and fun. What I did come up with, with my coach at the time, was this idea of getting conscious around money. It wasn't necessarily about changing or cutting back; it was just about becoming more aware, without judgment, and then taking it from there. The thing is, when you discover you spent more than $50 on coffee in one month, it's hard not to make a decision to cut down the cappuccino intake.

If you want to do this, too, go through last month's bank statement (there are also a number of apps that will help you track your purchases). Have an open, accepting mind—don't judge yourself for the past (or cry over spilled milk). You can feel proud of yourself for doing this.

Get out your highlighters and start grouping things together. Maybe you pick one color for bills—as well as rent or mortgage, you might include other monthly expenses like energy, cell phone, internet, insurance, etc.

You could also underline and color-coordinate transport, then food, then subscriptions (charities, Netflix, Spotify, etc.). There will still be some things left over. Look at all the transactions over $20. (If you are a big spender, you might want to make this more.) Can you separate them into groups? Perhaps going out, or health—massages, gym membership?

Once you've got these groupings, you begin to get a clearer picture of where the money is going. Decide what you want to do about that. I realized I was hemorrhaging a lot of money on cheap taxis. I discussed it with my coach, and we decided that I would set up a separate account into which I could put money when I chose to get the bus instead of a taxi—so I put the price of an Uber in the new bank account. It was far more rewarding to do it like that—it actually felt as though I was *earning* money, rather than cutting back. You can do this too—putting the price of a latte in your savings account when you go past a coffee shop and don't buy one!

Purpose

Finding your purpose is a somewhat grandiose term. Endeavoring to answer the question "What's your purpose?" can feel like trying to catch a cloud. That's why a lot of us give up on the whole concept—where philosophers and prophets have fought and failed, why should we mere mortals be any more fruitful? And anyway—what's the point?

That's a very important question, actually: What's the point? Or what's *our* point? As humans and as individuals? There are many schools of thought about what, as humans, our purpose is. In many monotheistic religions (Christianity, Islam, Judaism), the reason for being is to worship God and to do His will—and that worship is expressed by living in accordance with what the scriptures of those religions advise (and that's where the arguments start again).

Buddhism teaches that the purpose of life is to end suffering. Nice one, but again, there are a few different suggestions about how to do that (apparently, even Buddhists aren't all of one mind on this topic). There are some who subscribe to the notion that it is our purpose to have children—to breed and sustain the human race. I'm not a big fan of that one because I have a womb and I'd rather it didn't get too _The Handmaid's Tale_ anytime soon. Or perhaps it is love for all, or developing total compassion, which is our purpose. The quest for wisdom, truth, and knowledge show up a lot as something from which we could derive purpose, as well as helping others and making the world a better place to live. Some rate physical pleasure high on the meaningful list—others say it is merely a distraction from achieving a greater state of consciousness: transcending our bodily urges. Nihilists say that there is no purpose to life; it is essentially meaningless. Or that we have to create our own. I quite enjoy the boldly brutal stance of Chinese Legalism on the matter, which states it is meaningless even to look for meaning in human existence and all activity should be directed toward increasing the power of the ruler and wealth of the state. Happy days.

When I'm talking about purpose, I'm talking about what gives you meaning in life. I'm talking about why you think you are here on this Earth and what you are choosing to spend that time doing. But why care at all? Especially if evolution means we are just randomly plonked here by chance.

Well, it seems that there is scientific evidence that shows we do care: Having purpose is good for our health. Eudaemonic happiness (a type of happiness linked to meaning, rather than simply pleasure) was linked to lower levels of inflammatory gene expression and higher levels of antibody and antiviral genes. A large study in *The Lancet* found that a sense of purpose and meaning was linked to a longer life.[34] Purpose in life is linked to cognitive function—especially as we age. Additionally, people who believe there is meaning to life sleep better.[35]

But if random evolution means we are only here by accident, then aren't we searching for something that doesn't exist? Possibly—it depends how you think about it. If you are just here by accident, think about how remarkable that is. It's pretty extraordinary. Perhaps your purpose, then, is really to inhabit this body that you accidentally adopted, to be here as much as possible—as alive and incarnate as you can on this physical Earth, whatever making the most of a chance occurrence looks like to you. You might win the lottery simply because of the luck of the draw, but that doesn't mean that you should spend the money like it is has no value.

Having purpose, to me, means living a meaningful life, an existence filled to the brim with value—you find value in what you do and experience, you feel you are valuable, you are in touch with what you value in others, and you act in accordance with what you value. We all have days when we don't feel like that sometimes, when we feel like hiding under a blanket with a dog or a cat or a cheesecake or all three, but that's the intention.

And intention it is. Finding purpose is not the same as achievement, although it may express itself along the way as accomplishing certain things. Achieving is about doing things. Purpose is more of a way of being. The word comes from the twelfth-century Old French *porpos*, meaning aim or intention, and further back from the Latin root of *por*, meaning forth. I think of purpose as the way we move forward—how we go forth. Purpose is a kind of energetic navigation—it decides the way we're pointing and provides the drive to take the first step. I think of purpose as being a kind of North Star on steroids.

If you're aware that you don't have a sense of meaning, it can feel disorienting. You may feel restless a lot, or as though you're just drifting from one project to another, with no idea why you are doing what you are doing and feeling bad about that. Even when you are moving in a certain direction, you may feel as though you're just going through the motions, for no real reason that moves you, other than that you have no idea what else to do, or that the other options look worse. You don't feel depressed as such, but there's this low-level dissatisfaction about your life that nags at you whenever you stop what you're doing long enough to notice it. You might mask it in busyness, to prevent the feeling from arising. When you don't have a sense of purpose, then comfort becomes your top priority and any sort of suffering and challenge is to be avoided, as it feels pointless.

Some people get very anxious about finding their purpose, for some or all of these reasons. They feel they must live up to their full potential—anything less than that is a waste of their life—and that having a purpose looks a certain way, or that a person with purpose is successful in all the ways we sometimes value success in this world. For me, purpose is about learning to be yourself as much as possible—and sometimes that's not a case of doing, but of letting go of all the things that aren't yours. Some clients come to me for coaching to help them find their purpose and talk about it as some sort of macho intrepid mission. It's not about toughening up and pushing through, but about slowing down and being willing to let go.

See, uncovering what is meaningful for us and acting in accordance with that is more like learning a vulnerable art of undressing, except instead of peeling off our clothes we're removing all the dirt and sludge we've become smothered in over the years, some of which was thrown at us, some of which we fell into by accident, and some of which we grabbed willingly to protect our precious little inner being inside.

In Jamie Catto's book, *Insanely Gifted*, he tells a story of the artistic process of becoming and giving from another perspective: "When they asked Michelangelo about his epic David sculpture, he said that as soon as they brought him the huge slab of rock he could see the figure of David standing there within. His job was just to chip away the excess marble . . . ."[36]

Finding purpose is mostly a process of de-armoring, lifting off our outdated protections, so that we can rediscover the beauty we have inside us, let it shine out, and share it with the world. Then we can breathe more easily, hear more clearly, and feel more precisely, and it's easier to get in touch with that voice we haven't been able to hear over all the outside conditioning, the work directives, the media, the family messages, the angry exes, the fear, the shoulds, the shouldn'ts, the have-tos, and the musts. Deep down, we all know what the next right step is at any one time. It's just that the way we've been living our lives means we can't hear the voice that tells us anymore. Somewhere, years ago, we ignored it, because it told us to do something inconvenient, difficult, or painful, and we silenced it and repressed it until it got so quiet we have no idea what it sounds like any more. You know the voice—it sometimes tells us, "I want to go now," or "I like that; give me more of that," or "That hurts now—no more." It's the one that sometimes says, "I really want to kiss him," or "Cancel it—I don't want to do it," or "Go this way," even when the way it points is dark and scary and you have no idea where it leads.

Sometimes, what feels like our purpose clashes with what our parents wanted for us or the sort of thing we feel we should do. Maybe we've spent years studying to be an architect, only to find we love watercolors. Or we've bought a beautiful home and have a wonderful family, but our heart wants to travel. We can't see how to move forward, without breaking other people's hearts or our own. It can be agonizing, but the only thing to do is surrender and admit to yourself that you hear the voice and you are willing to follow it, even if you can't see what to do right now.

There's a beautiful bit in Mark Nepo's *The Little Book of Awakening* where he tells the story of his friend Robert, who was carrying gallons of red paint into his house after mixing it outside, with a brush in his mouth and cloth under his arm.[37] He didn't want to put everything down to open the door and so did an awkward shuffle and almost went inside. "I lost my grip, stumbled backward, and wound up on the ground, red gallons all over me," Robert tells Nepo.

This incident makes Nepo muse on how we all do something similar in life—not with paint, but with our emotional baggage—and the stories we carry about our past or our future, or even ourselves. Sometimes in order to move through the next door, to take advantage of the openings that appear in our lives, we have to let things go. We have to put down what we are carrying if we want to cross the threshold. Finding your purpose can be a bit like that. A case of removing all that you are holding onto that isn't really part of you, so you not only know which door is the right one to open but can make your way through it.

We'll have lots of doors to choose from, and they might be the right door one day and the wrong door the next. To talk about finding your life purpose is a bit of a misnomer. It suggests that you can only have one purpose and if you're not 100 percent sure what it is, well then, you're wasting your precious time here on Earth, until you find it out and devote your life to it. In my opinion, you can have lots of different purposes—your job is only to find what gives you purpose, or the direction you should move in, right now. That's as much as you can ever know. We're all constantly changing and adapting. Let's not shackle our souls to any one thing for the rest of our lives just because it's a Sunday afternoon and we're in the grip of an existential panic about not being worthwhile or having a bit of a raggedy résumé.

For me, purpose is not something that arrives from outside but is more a question of what your relationship to yourself and the wider world is at any one time. It changes with you, it's fluid, and there can/should be no pain in that, because every lesson is valuable. Living with purpose is a way of relating to your experiences, so that moving through pain and discomfort is worthwhile, rather than something to be avoided, because you can use what you've learned to help others in the same situation. If you can face your challenges consciously and work out how to get through them—on your own or with the help of others—then when someone else like you (for there are many) comes up against the same struggle, you can lead the way for them. This is how we can approach pain, grief, and hurt lovingly.

I've learned that "being in your purpose" or "living your purpose"—to use somewhat grandiose terminology—is really just a matter of answering yes to at least two of these three things at any one time. The first is about learning: Are you growing or pushing yourself in some way? Are you progressing? The second is about enjoyment or feelings: Do you find your life satisfying? Is it fulfilling? The third is about your relationship to others and the wider world: Are you able to share what you are learning? Are you helping others? Psychiatrist David Viscott wrote in his book *Finding*

Your Strength in Difficult Times: A Book of Meditations: "The purpose of life is to discover your gift. The work of life is to develop it. The meaning of life is to give your gift away."[38]

Help! I Can't Hear My Inner Voice

Suggesting "tuning into your inner voice" is deeply unhelpful advice for anyone experiencing a rough patch in their lives. A bit irritated was how I felt when people spoke to me about inspiration and finding purpose when I worked in a dark newsroom with anxiety-inducing targets all day. "I'll find my goddamn purpose when I have time," I grumbled inwardly.

If you feel the same, I have one piece of advice for you. Slow down. Delegate. Start saying no. Plan nothingness. Hours in your week where you don't do things; you just get there and then decide how you feel. In the morning, at lunchtime, after work, ask yourself: "How do I feel?" and "What does my body want right now?"

Slowing down will be uncomfortable because you've been racing at that speed for so long, it's unnerving to change velocity. There's a sailing term, "land sickness," which relates to when you are onboard a boat for days and the weather's rough but your sea legs are sturdy; people might be puking over the side, but you've got this, no problem (damn landlubbers). Then you anchor up, or come ashore, walk off the boat, and, oh, dear Lord, that's when the motion sickness kicks in. You have to take seasickness tablets to stop the nausea of returning to stability.

This happens when we slow down sometimes. It feels bad. We might blame slowing down for being the problem, but really it's the disruptive motion of our old lives that's still in our bodily rhythms.

Plus, when we slow down we begin to feel all the not-so-nice things we hadn't felt because of the distracting motion in our old lives—anger, grief, or loneliness. Being misunderstood or hurt. Give yourself full approval for where you are. Accept that feeling such pain is part of getting rid of it. It helps. It's a bit like a hangover. One of the reasons you feel like garbage is because, to process the alcohol, the liver initially has to convert the alcohol into something called acetaldehyde, which is joyfully toxic, and so you get a whole bunch of crappy symptoms like sweating, nausea, and vomiting. It means the alcohol is leaving your system and you're on your way to feeling better, but wow, it can feel rough.

Once you're in that slower space, and the fog is clearing, it's possible to start taking a better look at who you are and how you might want to engage with the world. But first, simply send yourself a bit of love and gratitude, because asking "What am I here on Earth for? What can I do?" is a beautifully awake and alert question, bursting with humanity.

Aside from slowing down, there are a few other things you can try to help point you in the right direction:

★ Write down all the skills you think you have.
★ Then ask a friend: "If you were going to come for me for help on one thing, what would it be?" Or ask: "If you were going to recommend me to someone for something, what would it be?" (Another question you could ask is

"What do you appreciate about me?" This can also show you what you have to offer.)

★ Next, write down all the difficult things you have gone through. This is a list you may be able to use to empathize with others and support them through their own difficult things. How could you help other people in the same situation?

★ Think about things that you find fulfilling. List them. If there aren't many, think about some things that you want to try.

Sit with this new knowledge of where you already provide meaning and how you could provide more. Don't get hung up on it, but simply commit to being curious and slowing down enough to follow what feels right.

Your Worldview

Deep below the surface of our being—in that ocean of dreams, memories, and buried feelings—there abides a patient captain, sitting at the bridge of a submarine.

We don't always know she's there, apart from when the vessel is moved, maybe by music, a baby laughing, a beautiful landscape, or a marriage ceremony.

Sometimes the waters are rocked by more painful vibrations—when we witness disasters on the news, when we lose a loved one, when we fail or watch others crumple through the same disappointment—times we are betrayed and in the freedom of forgiveness.

At such moments, we sense movement under the waters: The captain has called the crew into action, the propellers judder into life, and suddenly we realize there may be something else that can power our thoughts, feelings, and behavior other than bold rationality, the hustling to-do list, the routine triumphs and mundane irritants that dominate our daily life.

We may not be able to identify or label what is stirred ... but we know it in a mystical sense: that there is something deep and strong and pure moving within us, and it has us cast around with fresh eyes, as if we've peeled back a film from our existence, and are being asked to engage with something more true—those big questions, questions we don't often ask and sometimes completely refuse to. I think there are five big ones:

1. What is the nature of humanity—are we good or bad or neither?
2. Why is there so much suffering?
3. What is our relationship to the universe—and this planet?
4. What happens after we die?
5. What is love?

These questions are so vital and the answers so unverifiable that they often scare us. They require us to trust in our felt sense as humans, not in our names or our degree results, our salaries or our looks. Sometimes, the very prospect of engaging with this is too much, so we refuse to acknowledge these moments at all, afraid that the movement in the waters will persist and grow, until our very ocean floor trembles with a power that cannot be ignored. Yet calmly, gently, persistently, and in a deafening whisper, these questions ask us to upend our lives. To think differently, feel differently, act differently. It points our existence in an entirely different direction.

This subterranean navigation system is our worldview, and the captain guides us based on our beliefs. She is the most powerful commander of our souls and yet is completely surrendered to us, too, and waits patiently to see whether we will heed the call to engage with the invisible waters beneath us as they move. If we do, we can experience moments of joy and of pain and move forward in a way that best honors ourselves and the world.

When we don't, when we choose numbness over feeling, we can't access those spiritual moments of truth. Deaf and drowsy, we choose to live on the choppy surface, tossed around by wave after wave of superficial distractions. We can spend years, whole lifetimes, ignorant of these depths, and our captain, sad but devoted, sits on the bridge, waiting for us to wake up, as we waft through life, rudderless and restless, searching the horizon for something to direct us from the outside, rather than from within.

However, just because we don't examine these guiding beliefs doesn't mean the submariner goes to sleep. Our worldview doesn't stop influencing our thoughts, feelings, and behavior. Ignorant of the depths, however, our worldview gets hijacked by the everyday—the school bully, the abusive comment on Instagram, the angry manager, the cheating spouse—by rejection, by prejudice, by cultural conformity, by religious dogma.

We allow the world to shape us, rather than us shaping our world. When that happens, certain beliefs can hold us back, trapping us in a view of self and other that strangles life's infinite possibilities before we even realize what they could be.

I'm using "worldview" to mean beliefs about the world, in particular the things we can't see—the as-yet-unknown or the unknowable. It's what philosophers call the metaphysical. This both influences, and is influenced by, our relationship to the world, yet often it's so automatic, we don't consider what's powering it—and, by association, steering us.

Believe It, Then You'll See It

The first thing you have to do is believe in the power of belief. Believe that it can change your world. At the very least, be willing *to suspend your doubt* in the power of belief. Just for this section, banish from your mind the phrase "I'll believe it when I see it." It's the silliest phrase ever. Believe it, *then* you'll see it. That's the way the world works, most of the time. And it's why our beliefs about the world are so important.

Our beliefs are paintbrushes and pencils that draw and color the landscape in front of us. They decide the topography of our reality. What we believe about adversity can transform the challenges we face in life, from a barefoot slog over the volcanic plains of Mordor to a sweaty but enjoyable hike through Elysium.

If we have a hopeful view of humanity, we can become agile climbers rather than static spectators. Whether we see the back of the traveler in front of us or the stars in the sky, depends on how far we can see. Whether we see the world as a battlefield strewn with bloodied bodies, or as dominated by oceans covering its surface, washing us all clean, depends on whether we are zooming in or zooming out. How we see trees changes whether we hug them or chop them down, whether we plant or consume.

So what makes for a helpful belief versus an unhelpful one? It seems the first attribute is making sure that your belief is flexible and acknowledges a changing, adapting world. That means believing, like the ancient Greek philosopher Heraclitus did, in flux: People can change, physical circumstances can change, and emotional states can change. It's also helpful to have a flexible relationship with your beliefs (being open-minded) and to ensure that flexibility is built into them (thinking that the world must or should be a certain way is unhelpfully rigid).

Believing that people can change and improve actually helps them change and improve, according to research done by Stanford University psychologist Carol Dweck. She proposed the "growth mind-set" theory, which has been pivotal in changing the way we think about education and attainment.

As part of a series of experiments, she identified two main types of belief that even younger children have about their intelligence. There's the "fixed mind-set," which, for example, is when you believe that intelligence is something you are born with, and all you can do is uncover this innate gift. If you have a malleable view, you believe you can improve your intelligence and change. Her research showed that children with fixed theories about their intelligence struggled to improve their performance over the school year—and this was the case just as much for children with high IQs, who were praised for being bright.[39] When these kids experienced failure, they saw it as a sign that they had reached the limits of what they were good at—it wasn't something they could change, but a personal failing that couldn't be improved upon. This meant that not only were they much more adversely affected by it, but they didn't make as much effort attempting to learn anything to improve their skills.

Dweck's research found that children were similarly impacted by fixed beliefs about their personalities. If a child with a fixed view of their personality was rejected by one clique at school, they moved away and stopped trying to make new friends—even if there were ten other groups ready to welcome them. Because these children thought the problem was in them, they viewed this as evidence of something they couldn't do anything about. The difficulty with this is if children retreat when they are rejected, they don't learn social skills, and so their belief that they are fundamentally unlikable ends up seeming real.

A belief that our natures are fundamentally fixed affects adults too. Another study showed that if white people think racism is a fixed attribute—innate and unchangeable—they are likely to exhibit prejudiced behavior even if they aren't actually prejudiced. This would exhibit itself in not even wanting to engage in activities like learning about African-American history. The psychologists conducting the study suggested that despite not having racist beliefs, the white participants were worried about uncovering something they could not change, so they avoided situations with black people where their fears might be confirmed and were more resistant to activities that might reduce prejudice.

Another of Dweck's studies had college students fill in a questionnaire that ascertained whether they had fixed or malleable beliefs. When the students with fixed personalities experienced low moods, they were much less able to cope than those with more malleable beliefs about themselves, whose ability to cope was actually boosted by such moments, which encouraged them to build new skills, problem-solve, and seek out different ways of thinking or feeling.[40]

Whether or not we believe we can cope with adversity actually affects whether or not we can cope with adversity. This is the premise of a type of psychological therapy called Rational Emotive Behavior Therapy (REBT), and it's based on the idea that it's not the event that causes psychological disturbance in people but the irrational and unhelpful beliefs that are triggered by them. Albert Ellis, who developed the system, was influenced by Epictetus in the *Enchiridion*, who wrote: "Men are disturbed not by things, but by the views which they take of them."

If we believe we are ever-expanding human beings who can cope, learn, and improve—if we see our challenges as difficult but not impossible, then everything seems that little bit brighter, and we carry a candle of hope with us, even when it gets dark. This expansive attitude means that we are able to seek out those things that will help us to improve. Mountains are not there to show us how small we are but to teach us how to climb.

This last bit is crucial and is where a lot of positive thinkers go awry, in my humble opinion. Believing you can overcome your low mood doesn't, automatically, mean that your mood will magically improve. What it means is that you've created an opportunity to look at and look for ways to improve your mood, and you may find some (a caveat to this is that it is not a stick to beat yourself over the head with when you're struggling to feel better).

Ser and Estar

In Spanish, there are two words meaning "to be": *ser* and *estar*—but they mean slightly different things. One is permanent (*ser*) and one is temporary (*estar*). We might be fat right now, but we're not fat—it's just a temporary condition. We might be anxious right now, but we aren't anxious people. That isn't actually us. "Right now" is your best friend when it comes to putting things in perspective: You don't know what to do right now, you don't know how you feel about this right now, you're scared right now. Things change, and so will you and your feelings.

Believing that you will be good at astrophysics doesn't make you good at astrophysics, but if you want to become an astrophysicist and trust that you have the capacity, then you will need to find a teacher, and do the things that someone who wanted to learn astrophysics would do, rather than stay in the same old job, doing the same old thing.

Belief, in this sense, is not an instruction manual, but a pair of glasses that lets you read the instruction manual better, or see that there's been one in the box the whole time.

Pain, Adversity, Humanity

My experience of adversity (also known by other aliases—suffering, pain, despair, disaster, sickness, anxiety, distress, misery) has been powerfully altered over the last two years. It's not made life any less painful or turbulent. In twelve months, I quit my job, started a business, lost two grandparents, suffered from periods of depression, and saw a friend die by suicide. At times, it has felt excruciating—but somehow my beliefs about pain, struggle, and our capacity as humans to transcend and be transformed by adversity have shifted me to a place where I can *feel* them but they don't break me. Some of these painful experiences did see parts of my life change—but these parts were already broken. Some of them saw whole chunks of me fall off—the workaholic, the heavy drinker, the sarcastic one, the busy one—but those parts of me needed to go. I'm not a chemist, and I'm not heavily religious, but there's a helpful metaphor in the Bible that draws on both disciplines. It's repeated a lot, but the basic principle is most obviously stated in Isaiah 48:10 when God says, "Behold, I have refined you, but not as silver; I have tried you in the furnace of affliction."

Gold gets harder and stronger when it's heated to high temperatures. When silver is heated, it separates from any impurities. In this way, painful experiences can help show you more of what is true, if you let them. Suffering is the place where you find and develop compassion for others. It's a horrible, cosmic joke, but being terrified is the only place you can discover or develop courage. Being hurt or wounded is the only way you'll have an opportunity to let go or forgive. It's easy to be a good person when everything is wonderful, but it's powerful to be a good person when the chips are down.

> When melons are under stressful climate conditions, there is an increase in sugar, as they try to survive, and they end up being much more delicious. Heatwaves cause higher rates of photosynthesis in peaches, which means the sugar levels increase in the fruit. Peaches ripen earlier and are extra sweet when things get hot.

I like the word adversity to describe pain or suffering, because the thing about adversity is that you meet it and face it. Adversity has a curious etymology—it originally comes from the Latin word *advertere*, meaning to "turn toward," "to face," or "to confront," as if the instructions for how to handle adversity were contained within the word itself. We turn toward the pain, and that is the only way we can know how to overcome it.

Adversity is the place that teaches you skills to be a better human. Maybe you can empathize with and help someone else who finds themselves in a hole and thinks they're the first one to land there. They'll have to climb the ladder on their own, but you can at least direct them to where the ladder is, so they know that they are not alone and that there is a way out.

When it feels too much, just know that the world is always changing. Have you ever tried to string out a good feeling or hold onto happiness forever? Yup, you can't, as anyone who has ever attempted to go on a daylong date will know. The same is true of pain. It doesn't burn with the same intensity forever. Something good will come of it if you sit with it and allow it to soften your heart. Something good will come of it if you make sure it does.

Reality Check

A note here, because I think this is all well and good to say when you're not drowning in the eye of a hideous hurricane of suffering. When you are, it's just sobbing into your pillow, wailing, "I'm learning nothing, there is no point to this, it's just awful, and life is terrible."

A silly example of this (that did not feel silly at all at the time) is when I was panicking one day about a story deadline and my friend, also replete with precious-metal metaphors, told me, "Diamonds are formed under pressure."

I looked at her, my eyes bursting from lack of sleep and five coffees before 9 a.m., my tongue furry and feral, and replied somewhat sarcastically, "Are they actually? Because right now I'm just experiencing extreme anxiety."

What I did learn that day, after reaching diamond-forming point (my computer decided to install all its updates in a two-hour reboot and I burst into tears on the phone to a friend), is that I needed to be a bit nicer to myself. When lessons aren't coming, and you're still in pain, just pour a bit of love over yourself. Cancel the things you don't need to do. Call a friend. Breathe in and breathe out, with one hand on your heart and one hand on your belly. Stroke a dog/cat/tree/partner. Get into nature. Do the things that soothe you.

Be kind to your sweet, lovely self. Everything will do as it will do. There are some kinds of suffering that call for learning, conquering, being brave, opening up, and being vulnerable. Other times—and, actually, if I'm honest, at all times—the moment calls for us to be tender, caring, and loving to ourselves.

If all else fails, see if you can find some laughter. This one time I had a bout of terrible depression and couldn't leave the house. I ordered a weird combination of food to my door and half-heartedly ate it before leaving it by the bed. Then my friend came over to see me and, getting up to go to the door, I put my bare foot in a whole load of sweet-and-sour chicken and burst into tears. I opened the door sobbing and my friend was desperately asking, "What's wrong?" I pointed to all the sauce on my foot and wailed that I had stepped in food, and she sort of looked at it in horror and then looked at me, with a kind of "I don't know what the right thing to say about this is" expression, and came up with "It could be quite moisturizing."

This attempt at consolation was so weird and untrue and useless that I just said, "It's not." And then we both began to laugh.

Zoom In and Out

Playing with perspective is one way to shift your worldview so that it helps you navigate your feelings and behavior better. I think of it as zooming in or zooming out. Are you looking at one small part of life, or are you looking at the whole? Which is most helpful?

For example, a series of terrible events can happen, and it can fracture our view of the world, if we zoom in and focus just on this. But if we expand our worldview, and if we open our hearts to seeing the good things, too, then often it can feel a little less painful.

Mark Nepo relates a parable in his *The Little Book of Awakening*. It's about a Hindu master who, fed up with his complaining apprentice, decides to teach him a lesson.

The Hindu master asks his apprentice to put a handful of salt into a glass of water and drink it. As the apprentice spits it out, the master asks, "How does it taste?"

To which the young man replies, "Bitter."

The two of them then walk to the nearby lake, where the Hindu master asks the apprentice to put another handful of salt in. He then instructs him to take a cup and drink from the lake. "How does it taste now?" he asks his young charge.

"Fresh," the apprentice replies.

The moral of the story (health and safety concerns aside) is that our pain will feel as concentrated as the container it is held in. It's not really about getting rid of pain—pain in life is there and will always be there. Nepo writes: "So when you are in pain, the only thing you can do is to enlarge your sense of things . . . Stop being a glass. Become a lake."

Becoming a lake begins by realizing, when I'm down or feeling stressed, that there is someone in the world feeling just like me right now. Probably even within a fifty-mile radius, someone a bit like me, going through the exact same thing, having the exact same feelings.

Expanding my world means looking at old things. I live in London, and I like looking at historic buildings. When I look at St. Paul's, I think it's so beautiful and inspiring: how the architect and everyone else who came together to make it for us all are now just dirt and bones and old reported bits of history. And how someone else is going to come along, and have the same semiprofound thought, when this building is still standing and I am dead.

Zooming out means pausing for fifteen seconds and looking at the sky, and the clouds going past, and knowing that I have no control over them. I let my smallness soothe me, and feel hopeful, knowing that there's so much I don't know and that maybe it will all be okay, and that if it's not there's very little I can do about it, other than surrender to that sense of mystery and dream big.

At other times, it's helpful for me to zoom in, to focus solely on what is in front of my face, what I can see, hear, and touch physically. I remember that one time I had a huge project to complete, and halfway through, I felt exhausted, I just couldn't see how I would ever get it done. That was a time when I zoomed in, and simply focused on what I had to do in the next hour, and then the next day, and then the next month.

Ernest Hemingway had great advice for writers: "All you have to do is write one true sentence. Write the truest sentence that you know." There's something about doing this that feels possible. And once you do that possible thing, you look back and think, "Okay, I did that one; maybe I can do the next one."

One breath at a time. One step at a time. One self-loving thought at a time. Just looking at what's in front of you. Then repeating that process until, somewhere along the way, you realize you've traveled a little further than you thought you could, and you begin to believe.

Love, Death, Pain, Humanity, and God

What you come to believe about the world from the experiences and emotions that stir your own inner submariner are unique to you. We all have our own worldview—it's about becoming actively conscious of yours, so that you aren't navigating blind. I've also suggested some methods for setting your compass so that it functions more effectively for you—being flexible with your beliefs, knowing that both circumstances and you can change, not seeing pain as a punishment but more as an opportunity for growth—zooming in and zooming out when you need some space to breathe and a more helpful perspective.

As for my own beliefs? Well, here's how I see it.

Death: This is how we change form. Matter can't be destroyed. Things only ever change state.

Love: This is how much power we have.

Pain: This is how we learn courage, compassion, and acceptance.

Humanity: The only thing we need to believe in is our capacity for change.

God/Higher Power: This is what teaches you how to let go with love. To surrender to what is and simply trust. It is the relationship to the other four combined, but more than that: to hope, goodness, and the best you can imagine. The relationship to a higher power comes before everything else.

Plugging Into the Bigger Picture

Care about the world. You need it, and it needs you. Your invitation is this—to care for and value your own life so that you can care for and value the life of the planet. To treat the lives of others with loving-kindness and be constantly reminded to be sweet and gentle with yourself, too, because we all share in and are made of the same magic.

At first, caring in this way might feel a bit shaky—a stop-start process as you fill up your energy pot (take care of yourself) and pour out from it (offer to others). As you relax a bit more, you'll see it's more about letting yourself be a sieve. If you can trust enough to open yourself up and expand your perspective to a greater vision, you'll be able to let more of the world in to nourish you (it really wants to). The "filling up" process becomes automatic (joy is everywhere, waiting to refresh us), and you'll never get to the bottom of your resources, or need to stop and seek for ways to fill up your pot, to grasp for energy unhelpfully or unhealthily, using the world or people instead of experiencing them.

You won't have to expend effort as you pour it out either, but rather can just continually let the natural flow happen. It doesn't require you to do or control; it just requires you to listen to the bigger thing, realize that you're part of it, and allow your caring to be plugged into that.

It's about seeing the joy that's present and available to us when we open our eyes to the wider world—and sweeping away anything in the way. Sometimes you might be able to do this by meeting your obstacle with a smile and open heart. Other times, the impediments in our path will only dissolve through tears. It doesn't matter whether suffering or good fortune is your route; both are part of living. Just know that peace and joy lie underneath everything. There's more of it than you could imagine. So much so that, once you've found it, you'll want to share it with everyone.

It Doesn't Mean Sacrificing Your Life

I've been talking about giving a f★★k about causes, projects, purpose, service; these are all grand words, but whatever you care about doesn't need to be impressive in any historical sense. What I really mean is: Care about something that society, self-reliance, or compliance doesn't "require" you to. Something of your own choosing, that arises from a desire within. It can be litter-picking, teaching, singing, cooking, writing, nursing, dancing. It doesn't have to be curing world hunger or malaria. In fact, get the idea of "cure" out of your head completely.

The world doesn't need saving, and neither do you. We've just been a little bit sleepy, blurry-eyed, and forgetful, that's all. Unfortunately, like anyone who has slept past their alarm, there's a tendency for us, upon waking up, to look around and panic. No time to enjoy a coffee or a croissant, because we're very late, and there's a lot to do. We look at that world in this urgent headspace and think, "Oh, God, there's mess and pain everywhere and there's so much to do and we must do it all ourselves and it's terrible and let's just throw ourselves into any activity at all, because everything is broken and desperately needs to be fixed."

There are lots of people who will tell you this. Some will be salespeople, who for the most part are faking this attitude. Others will be politicians, some of whom are also excellent actors and some of whom are genuinely sincere in their belief that action must be taken *now* and with a spirit of urgency and everyone is needed. There will be very well-meaning people who work for charities, who are totally earnest and are ready to sacrifice their lives for a cause. All these people and more will tell you how desperately important their thing is. Journalists, in particular, are a big fan of this. Ooh, and religious leaders. People with petitions. All in all, this merry band of vocational issue junkies will impress upon you, with utmost emergency, how deeply they need you to do a certain thing or another. How time is running out. They are not quite wrong, but they aren't right either. And they do themselves a disservice with their seriousness. They besmirch the good name of caring. Give and help if you want to, but do not get sucked into this facsimile of caring for things you know deep down aren't that important to you. Listen to your submariner first, then decide on all other extraneous chatter. Also—nothing comes at any cost.

No cause is worth sacrificing your precious life for—taking your attention off the whole, the bigger picture, and zooming in to channel all your energy into one thing, to the exclusion of all others. I'm not just referring to dramatic religious martyrdom. We forfeit our existence in many dull and dreary ways: decades in a job we hate, climbing a career ladder, mindlessly devoting ourselves to some vague sense of duty, paying off the mortgage, pouring all our energy into a relationship or raising a family. Quite often we dress the dishonorable devaluation of our own life in a cloak of virtue, wantonly wasting precious energy in support of some campaign, movement, political party, or charity.

In the short term, this can be a way of hiding from ourselves. In the long term, it's a form of abandoning the intrinsic value of our own life. It's ignorant—it's almost as if we are trying to prove the worthiness of our existence when we're already here, already existing, already enough. It's arrogant—as if there is something we could do with our heads or our hands that could in any way match how breathtakingly special it is that we happen to be alive.

We can commit to projects, become engaged and absorbed in a cause or a certain subject of interest, but when what you're *doing* becomes more important than how you are *being*, take a deep breath and come back to yourself. This is it, and it's spectacular in its simplicity. You can sit here and contemplate yourself and your amazing body; it's wonderful to simply be. Let your shoulders sink down. Feel the space in your chest expand. Let your jaw soften and the skin settle around your eyes. Feel the movements and rhythms in your body. See if you can notice any emotions. Look around you. The experience of this innate magic we have inside us, which comes from a bigger source, is your "why," not some nebulous striving to defeat the bad. If defeating evil is our purpose, then we'll just continue to make more evil, because otherwise we'll run out of meaning.

Whole-y F**k

Sometimes, instead of the "what"—the bigger vision—we get stuck on the "how." This is getting distracted by logistics—which pose their own problem, don't get me wrong—but mechanics is actually just a lot of small things; it's not *the* big thing. It's possibly not even a thing at all, just a way of thinking. When I'm talking about plugging into something bigger, I'm talking about the whole world—the universe even. It's hard for us to think this way, especially if we are from a Western background. We really like to boil things down into their constituent parts, considering the whole as simply what you get accidentally when everything comes together, rather than adopting a more holistic view, as some East Asian philosophies do.

This fragmented way of thinking informs our everyday life—in fact it is so pervasive it can even affect how we look at images, which one study set out to prove. Researchers took American and Chinese students and showed them images—for example, a picture of a tiger in the forest—and then tracked their eye movements. American students tended to focus more on the central object, whereas the Chinese students looked around the whole picture, taking in the context.[41]

Theoretical physicist David Bohm, a contemporary of Albert Einstein, was led by his research in quantum mechanics to propose that the nature of reality was actually a coherent whole—not just a collection of parts. That at a subatomic level, everything is highly connected—more than most of us can even imagine. He believed that many of the world's divisions could be healed if we were to adjust our way of thinking toward a reality that is unbroken, coherent, harmonious. It's our fragmented way of thinking that makes us see the world as fragmented.[42]

It can boggle the mind a bit to imagine everything in the universe, ourselves included, overlapping and influencing each other, electrons knocking and boinging together, and everyone and everything so highly interconnected that the butterfly effect seems boring. We live in time, which means we like things orderly and linear, and we're used to separating things out to make sense of them, dividing them into mine and yours. That can be a useful way of operating. But that's all it is.

When I'm talking about plugging into something bigger, I'm not saying care about communities or the planet because these things are superior to you or that you are small and inconsequential. The opposite, in fact. I'm saying: Plug into this whole, this view of totality, and realize that the world would be incomplete without you and you would be incomplete without the world. Sometimes, realizing we are part of something greater (as well as acknowledging that we are also complete in our own right), we can also remember our own greatness. Seeing our life, not only as a wonderful whole in and of itself but also as part of a bigger whole, works as a reminder of who we really are, helping us to become and embody that. If this sounds spiritual, then you might be onto something. The etymology of the word "holy" comes from the word "whole."

Don't Do It to Get It; Do It to Become It

It's good to give a f**k, to want to make an impact on the world, but make sure it's about changing and not about being the agent of that change.

Making things better for the world of which you are a part, helping life on a planet that enables you to live, rooted in a belief that you are connected and part of a whole, is sustaining and nourishing.

Caring about creating something life-affirming is almost impossible if you make it *your* mission. You're separating yourself from others and the planet. Your ego will get in the way of what's needed to complete it, and in the meantime you risk not going about it in a way that's affirming to your life.

Making it personal means deadlines. We don't have very long on this planet, especially if we want to bask in the credit too. How terrible would it be if it's *your* project and you die before it's completed? Then your life will have amounted to nothing. You'll either have to rush and get anxious or make your project smaller. Much smaller, for you are less likely to ask for help or collaborate, and you'll push for credit over your creation.

Dedication will be hard—if you're doing it just for your own ego, then when times get tough, those self-interested voices will shout louder. The comfort addiction will kick in. However, if you are answering to something bigger, it will be easier to take a break, be kind, and then find the strength, the inspiration, to carry on. Let the reason, the very thing you are working for, refuel you, not self-congratulation or the glory that you may never win.

We want to be creating batons to pass on, not striving for completion. The goal is not the thing you want anyway. Think about climbing a mountain: It's not actually about getting to the top—not really—because what do you do once you've reached the summit? Climb back down again.

It's about who you become in the process of climbing that mountain. The levels of fitness you have to achieve. The money you have to raise. The friends you make. The new skills you have to learn. The dedication you need to commit to. The fear you have to overcome. The countries you travel to. The beautiful landscape you see. The differences you encounter. The pain you overcome. The sickness. The exhilaration. The dark nights and the bright mornings. The wondering why you signed up to do this in the first place, and carrying on anyway. Getting to the top—well, that's just something to tell people back home.

Giving a f★★k means being engaged, interested, and active both in life and in all that enables you to live. It's not actually about getting anywhere, though no doubt you'll find yourself in some interesting spots along the way, and achieving great things, if you're doing it right. It's not actually about trying to force through change, though I'd be very surprised if you didn't witness a single positive impact. It's about what giving a f★★k asks of you as a person. It asks of you every single thing that is listed in this book—and more.

If you want to care, you'll have to keep returning to the present moment, because focusing on the future all the time will blow your head off. Then, after a while, you'll realize just how much pleasure there is to be had, here, in this oft-underrated dimension called right now.

If you care, you'll have to attend to your feelings, because otherwise, my God, will they attend to you. You'll find yourself taking care of your body, and listening to its wisdom, because it allows you to love life with more ease. You'll want to be kind to yourself, and use your imagination to dream of the best things, because anxiety doesn't make you feel good, and it's outlived its use. There's something bigger to plug into. Learn what caring really means, by constantly attending to yourself, and what you need, noting what you do well and what went a bit wrong. Pay attention to each part of your life in turn, and really care about making it feel good.

Before journalism, before coaching, right out of university, I went to the South of France to work as a stewardess on superyachts—those massive gin palaces that sail around the Mediterranean (one had a golf course onboard and another had a submarine). The guests we served were immensely wealthy—I poured drinks, made the beds, and ironed the underpants of kings, celebrities, famous business tycoons, and political leaders. Millions of dollars were spent every day, thrown away as if money were as inconsequential as a toothpick. One lunch break I was sitting with a weathered deckhand at a port bar, expressing my amazement at the huge amounts of money floating around. He told me that, depending on how long these yacht owners had had their wealth, it altered how they spent it.

"These people get their money, and the first thing they do is play. They buy toys. That's what a lot of the people with yachts here are still doing. These are just toys for them."

He took a long drag of his cigarette and gestured with his hand to another boat in the harbor, which we knew a famous politician owned.

"Most of them, after a while, they get bored of just having money and playing around, and they want influence, so they go for power instead," the deckhand told me.

"That's why some of these people are leaders—they go into politics to try and feel better. Or they want fame—that's the other route they take. But the people who have had money for a while, or the people that have real money [in yachting that means billions and billions], they usually go into philanthropy."

I thought about it, and then went back to the boat to clean up condoms and champagne glasses from the VIP cabin (that guest was still on the play cycle, for sure). However, over ten years later, this conversation has stuck with me. Most of us never reach the immense sums of money that would have us wake up and realize that maybe money isn't everything. We never get to lead a country and realize that doesn't quite hit the spot either. And it takes billions and billions before people wake up and realize that actually, as humans, the thing we want is to do something of value that helps others.

Wouldn't it be great if we didn't need to be superyacht owners before we plugged into the bigger picture? Wouldn't it be great if we could just give a f**k about who we are, about the world we interact with every day, about things in the right order, in the right way? Wouldn't it be great if we could really give a f**k about each other, right now?

Acknowledgments

With thanks to my family and friends, who supported me throughout this process; to Naomi Langan, who helped me edit in the final week before my publisher's deadline, meaning I could meet it on time; and to the One Taste coaching program and everyone who taught in it— it was the trampoline for the research I did for this book and personal development in general. Thanks also to my editor, Emily Thomas, for being so supportive throughout this process, and to Peter Shiva, who taught me that this moment matters.

Notes

Yourself

1. This quote is disputed in origin but commonly attributed to Pierre Teilhard de Chardin. It was popularized by Wayne W. Dyer in his talks and Stephen Covey in his book *The 7 Habits of Highly Effective People*, both of whom attribute the words to him.

2. Csikszentmihalyi, M. (1997), *Finding Flow: The Psychology of Engagement with Everyday Life*, New York: Basic Books.

3. Kabat-Zinn, J. (2013), *Full Catastrophe Living*, New York: Bantam Books.

4. Robertson, I. (2018), *The Stress Test*, New York: Bloomsbury.

5. *The Guardian* (2013), "20 Amazing Facts about the Human Body." Available online at: https://www.theguardian.com/science/2013/jan/27/20-human-body-facts-science (accessed June 12, 2018).

6. Parkinson, C., and Lancaster, O. (1958), *Parkinson's Law*. London: John Murray.

7. Manning, Chelsea E. (2016), "Solitary Confinement Is 'No Touch' Torture, and It Must Be Abolished," *The Guardian*. Available online at: https://www.theguardian.com/world/commentisfree/2016/may/02/solitary-confinement-is-solitary-confinement-is-torture-6x9-cells-chelsea-manningno-touch-torture-and-it-must-be-abolished (accessed June 1, 2018).

8. Tillisch, K., Labus, J., Kilpatrick, L., Jiang, Z., Stains, J., Ebrat, B., Guyonnet, D., Legrain-Raspaud, S., Trotin, B., Naliboff, B., and Mayer, E.A. (2013), "Consumption of Fermented Milk Product with Probiotic Modulates Brain Activity," *Gastroenterology*, 144(7), pp. 1394–1401.e4.

9. Kuipers, Y., Emonts, M., Ten Brink, P., Mutafoglu, K., Schweitzer, J.-P., Kettunen, M., Twigger-Ross, C., Baker, J., Tyrväinen, L., Hujala, T., and Ojala, A. (2016), "The Health and Social Benefits of Nature and Biodiversity Protection," a report for the European Commission (ENV.B.3/ETU/2014/0039), Institute for European Environmental Policy, London/Brussels.

10. Bragg, R., and Atkins, G. (2016), "A Review of Nature-Based Interventions for Mental Health Care," Natural England Commissioned Reports, No. 204.

11. Fuentes, A. (2017), *The Creative Spark: How Imagination Made Humans Exceptional*, New York: Dutton.

12. Gamble, C. (2013), *Settling the Earth*, Cambridge: Cambridge University Press.

13. Robinson, K. (Sir Ken of TEDalot on Play and Learning), "PlayGroundology" (2012). Available online at: https://playgroundology.wordpress.com/2012/05/06/sir-ken-of-tedalot-on-play-and-learning/ (accessed May 31, 2018).

14. Vohs, K.D., Redden, J.P., and Rahinel, R. (2013), "Physical Order Produces Healthy Choices, Generosity, Conventionality, whereas Disorder Produces Creativity," *Psychological Science*, 24, 1714–21.

Relationships

15. Ngo, L. et al. (2015) "Two Distinct Moral Mechanisms for Ascribing and Denying Intentionality," *Scientific Reports*, 5, 17390; doi: 10.1038/srep17390.

16. Zitek, E.M., Jordan, A.H., Monin, B., and Leach, F.R. (2010), "Victim Entitlement to Behave Selfishly," *Journal of Personality and Social Psychology*, 98(2), 245–55.

17. Brené Brown, YouTube (2011), "The Power of Vulnerability." Available online at: https://www.youtube.com/watch?v=iCvmsMzlF7o&t=194s (accessed June 14, 2018).

18. Hobbes, T. (1904), *Leviathan: Or The Matter, Forme, & Power of a Common-Wealth Ecclesiasticall and Civill*, Cambridge: Cambridge University Press.

19. Lieberman, M. (2013), *Social: Why Our Brains Are Wired to Connect*, Oxford: Oxford University Press.

20. Nhs.uk. (2017), "Benefits of Love and Sex." Available at: https://www.nhs.uk/live-well/sexual-health/benefits-of-love-sex-relationships/ (accessed June 1, 2018).

21. Mech, L.D., Adams, L.G., Meier, T.J., Burch, J.W., and Dale, B.W. (1998), *The Wolves of Denali*, Minneapolis: University of Minnesota Press.

22. Ziglar, Z. (2012), *Secrets of Closing the Sale*, New York: MJF Books.

23. Maslow, A. (1943), "A Theory of Human Motivation," *Psychological Review*, 50(4), pp. 370–96.

24. Aesop (2018), *Aesop's Fables*, La Vergne: Dreamscape Media.

25. Burroughs, W. S. (1977), *Junky*, Penguin Books.

26. Carse, J. (1986), *Finite and Infinite Games*, New York: Ballantine Books.

27. Donovan, A. (2016), *Motivate Yourself: Get the Most out of Life, Find Purpose and Achieve Fulfilment*, West Sussex: John Wiley & Sons.

28. Association for Psychological Science (2011), "Why Do We Share Stories, News, and Information with Others?" Available online at: https://www.psychologicalscience.org/news/releases/why-do-we-share-our-feelings-with-others.html (accessed March 20, 2019).

29. Osho (2013), *Fear*, New York: St. Martin's Press.

30. Cacioppo, J.T., and Cacioppo, S. (2014), "Social Relationships and Health: The Toxic Effects of Perceived Social Isolation," *Social and Personality Psychology Compass*.

Infinity and Beyond

31. Taleb, N., and Chandler, D. (2007), *The Black Swan*, Prince Frederick, Maryland: Recorded Books.

32. Wattles, W. (2017), *The Science of Getting Rich*, La Vergne, Tennessee: Neeland Media LLC.

33. Ames, D. R., and Mason, M. F. (2015) "Tandem Anchoring: Informational and Politeness Effects of Range Offers in Social Exchange," *Journal of Personality and Social Psychology*, 108(2) (February 2015), pp. 254–74.

34. Steptoe, A., Deaton, A., and Stone, A. (2015), "Subjective Wellbeing, Health, and Ageing." *The Lancet*, 385(9968), pp. 640-648.

35. Lewis, N., Turiano, N., Payne, B., and Hill, P. (2016), "Purpose in Life and Cognitive Functioning in Adulthood," *Aging, Neuropsychology, and Cognition*, 24(6), pp. 662–71.

36. Catto, J. (2017), *Insanely Gifted: Turn Your Demons into Creative Rocket Fuel*, Edinburgh: Canongate Books Ltd.

37. Nepo, M. (2013), *The Little Book of Awakening*, Newburyport, Massachusetts: Red Wheel/Weiser.

38. Viscott, D. (2003), *Finding Your Strength in Difficult Times*. New York: McGraw-Hill Education.

39. Dweck, C.S. (2000), *Self-Theories: Their Role in Motivation, Personality, and Development*, Philadelphia: Psychology Press.

40. Molden, D., and Dweck, C. (2006), "Finding 'Meaning' in Psychology: A Lay Theories Approach to Self-Regulation, Social Perception, and Social Development," *American Psychologist*, 61(3).

41. Chua, H., Boland, J., and Nisbett, R. (2005), "From the Cover: Cultural Variation in Eye Movements during Scene Perception," *Proceedings of the National Academy of Sciences*, 102(35), pp. 12629–33.

42. Bohm, D. (2002), *Wholeness and the Implicate Order*, Hoboken, New Jersey: Routledge.